DAVID ABERCROMBIE

Studies in Phonetics & Linguistics

Oxford University Press

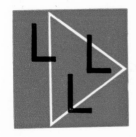

LANGUAGE AND LANGUAGE LEARNING | 10

Studies in Phonetics and Linguistics

LANGUAGE AND LANGUAGE LEARNING

General Editors: RONALD MACKIN *and* PETER STREVENS

Studies in phonetics and linguistics

DAVID ABERCROMBIE

London
OXFORD UNIVERSITY PRESS

Oxford University Press, Ely House, London W.1

GLASGOW   NEW YORK   TORONTO   MELBOURNE   WELLINGTON

CAPE TOWN   SALISBURY   IBADAN   NAIROBI   DAR ES SALAAM   LUSAKA   ADDIS ABABA

BOMBAY   CALCUTTA   MADRAS   KARACHI   LAHORE   DACCA

KUALA LUMPUR   SINGAPORE   HONG KONG   TOKYO

Library Edition ISBN 0 19 437117 4

Paperback Edition ISBN 0 19 437023 2

© Oxford University Press, 1965

First published 1965

Third impression 1971

Acknowledgements and thanks are due to the
following for permission to reprint copyright
material: Mouton and Co. (Ch. 3); the Philological
Society (Ch. 6); North-Holland Publishing Co.
(Ch. 7); Sir Isaac Pitman and Sons Ltd (Ch. 9);
Akademie-Verlag (Ch. 11 and 13); and the
International Phonetic Association (Ch. 15 and 16).

PRINTED IN GREAT BRITAIN BY HEADLEY BROTHERS LTD
109 KINGSWAY LONDON WC2 AND ASHFORD KENT

Preface

These studies in phonetics and linguistics consist of broadcasts and articles written on various occasions over quite a long period of time; they cover a span of twenty-eight years, in fact. That might seem bound to make them a somewhat random and heterogeneous collection. However, they do in fact represent a continuity of interest during this time in certain aspects of the two subjects, or more exactly, often, of the borderland between them: matters such as the functions of language in society, problems of writing and transcription, and the traditions of linguistic thought. The papers are not, therefore, arranged chronologically, but are roughly grouped according to topic. I have selected for inclusion papers which are not too technical or specialized, but are rather, I hope, of sufficient general interest to warrant their inclusion in a series such as this.

A collection of this sort is bound to involve some repetition. A certain amount of editing has been done in order to reduce the repetition as much as possible, but it is inevitable that some instances will remain, and for these I ask the reader's indulgence.

I am greatly indebted to Mr Peter McIntyre for compiling the index.

Edinburgh   DAVID ABERCROMBIE
1965

Contents

1

Conversation and spoken prose

1

In this paper I wish to discuss certain aspects of spoken language.

I am aware that the expression 'spoken language' is, in the opinion of many people, tautologous; it simply says the same thing twice. *All* language is spoken language, they would say; there is no such thing as written language, which is a contradiction in terms. I do not wish to argue about this here; I will simply say that, like many other students of linguistics, I hold strongly to the view that language can be manifested in writing just as well as in speech, and that I therefore look on the expression 'spoken language' as a reasonable and meaningful one.

Many different sorts of linguistic event come under the heading of spoken language, of course; such things, for instance, as:

making a speech,

giving a lecture (which is not the same thing as a speech),

gossiping with friends,

saying a prayer,

reading a news bulletin on the radio,

reciting poetry,

cross-examining a witness,

giving a commentary on a news-reel,

drilling a squad of soldiers,

acting in a play,

having an argument,

taking part in a panel discussion.

Evidently these are all different in various ways from each other. It seems to me, however, that all of them, and all other uses of

The first of a series of four public lectures on 'Spoken Language' given at the University of Ghana in February 1959. Published in *English Language Teaching*, Vol. XVIII, No. 1, 1963.

spoken language that you may be able to think of, fall into three broad categories. They can be described either as reading aloud, or as monologue, or as conversation. The distinction between these categories can obviously not be a hard-and-fast one, but in making it I am led to an important point. Let me first say a little more about the categories.

'Reading aloud' is a more common thing than at first one would suppose: apart from obvious instances, it includes most of radio speech (though very much less of TV speech). Under this heading one should include also the recitation by heart of something originally learnt from writing. We may note in passing that something which is read aloud may have been written in the first place for no other reason *than* to be read aloud. (The use of this first category of spoken language will necessarily be confined to literates.)

'Monologue' is the use of spontaneous spoken language, not prepared but created as it goes along, on those occasions when other people present, if any, are not *meant* to join in, whether in fact they do or not. Speeches, radio commentaries on sporting affairs, many lectures (other lectures would come into the category 'reading aloud') exemplify monologue. Included in this category may sometimes be events with the spurious appearance of conversation: a medieval disputation, for example, was really a succession of monologues.

Under 'conversation' I would include all those linguistic occasions when there is the *opportunity* for give and take; when it is understood that, at least in theory, there is more than one active participant, however long one of the participants may go on for.

Now, I would like to suggest that there is something *specialized* about the first two categories of uses of spoken language, 'reading aloud' and 'monologue'. Not everyone engages in them, or needs to, and certainly many who do engage in them fail to do so effectively. These two categories together would form a very small part of the sum total of instances of the use of spoken language which occur in the world. They have certain distinguishing linguistic, including phonetic, peculiarities, which set them off from other uses of spoken language. I believe that they have developed out of the category which I have called 'conversation'.

This last category, I would maintain, contains the most natural, the most frequent, and the most widespread occurrences of spoken language. All humans indulge in conversation, and the mind boggles at the volume of conversation that must occur in the world each day.

When we use the phrase 'spoken language' without further qualification, it is to conversation that we should be referring. The other uses of spoken language are adaptations, or specializations, of this basic category. This is the first point that I want to make.

2

Conversation itself, of course, takes the most varied forms: it may be between strangers, or between acquaintances, or between intimates; it may involve exchanging information, or merely exchanging goodwill—or perhaps ill-will. There are numerous formal differences to be found between these various kinds; but they all have certain basic characteristics in common.

Where can we find instances of these various kinds of conversation available for examination? Not, it is necessary to insist, in those places where at first thought it would seem most natural to find them, places where conversation might be expected to play a most important part: in novels, plays, and films. I should like in this connexion to refer to a point which Mr T. S. Eliot made in a lecture a few years ago.[1] He was defending the use of verse in the writing of drama, and he pointed out that though it is usual to distinguish two modes in which language is used, namely verse and prose, we ought really to distinguish three: verse, prose, and our ordinary speech. We have all heard (too often, as Eliot says) of Molière's character in *Le Bourgeois Gentilhomme* who was surprised to be told that he spoke prose: M. Jourdain was right to be surprised, because it was not true; he didn't speak prose—nobody does. Nobody *can*, or at least not for very long at a time. M. Jourdain only talked—and that, I hope to show, is something very different. Prose is essentially language organized for *visual* presentation.

---

[1] See *On Poetry and Poets* (London, 1957), p. 73.

Eliot's point was that it is just as artificial to make characters on the stage speak prose as to make them speak verse, and the latter needs no more defending than the former. But there is another point to be made from what he said. Most people believe that *spoken prose*, as I would like to call what we normally hear on the stage or screen, is at least not far removed, when well done, from the conversation of real life. Writers of novels are sometimes praised for 'naturalistic dialogue'; others, such as Miss Ivy Compton Burnett, are criticized because nobody speaks like the characters in their books.

But the truth is that nobody speaks at all like the characters in any novel, play or film. Life would be intolerable if they did; and novels, plays or films would be intolerable if the characters spoke as people do in life. Spoken prose is far more different from conversation than is usually realized.

We are constantly told that the main business of linguistics (and some would say its only business) is the investigation of spoken language; this is a point which has been especially strongly insisted on during the last 75 or so years. But what in fact linguistics has concerned itself with, up to now, has almost exclusively been— spoken prose. This is true of phonetics as well as all the rest of linguistics. Yet attention has seldom been drawn to this curious fact.

3

But is it true that conversation—ordinary talking—is *really* so very different from spoken prose? Eliot speaks of the former's 'fumbling for words, its constant recourse to approximation, its disorder and its unfinished sentences'. But the differences really go much deeper than that; they are not differences of degree, as Eliot seems to imply, but of kind. However, before we can discuss these differences, and show what conversation is really like, we still have the problem of obtaining specimens for examination—a real problem, because conversation is undoubtedly raw material which is as intractable to organize for investigation as could be.

There is really only one way of obtaining *genuine* conversation so that we can inspect and analyse it, and that is by rather a dubious technique: surreptitious, clandestine, recording. Only in the last ten years have machines been available which will do this adequately; but there is now no difficulty about it. No *mechanical* difficulty, that is: there is perhaps a moral difficulty. If a recording is to be of genuinely spontaneous conversation, those taking part in it must not suspect they are being recorded; so if you do record them, you are practising a deception on them. Of course, you can tell them afterwards; but there is still something distasteful about the procedure. It is possible, perhaps, to warn people that they are going to be recorded in the hope that after a while they will forget about the presence of the microphone; but they are bound to be conscious of it for a while, and the recording will inevitably be unnatural until they do forget.

However, a lot of material *has* been obtained in this way; and if one studies it carefully and listens to it from the 'outside' and not as one who took part in it, one soon realizes that the whole *structure* of conversation is different from that of prose, spoken or written. It comes as quite a surprise to find how different it is.

Ordinary listening to conversation does not bring this realization, and the surprise we feel when listening to recordings springs, I think, mainly from the fact that we are quite unused to listening to *disembodied voices* taking part in conversation. 'Invisible speech' is outside our normal experience. The participants are always physically present in ordinary conversation, and we can *see* them, and this visual participation changes the character of what we hear. When we listen to a recorded conversation taken away from its material context, we get a sudden 'outside' view of it.

On the other hand we are all nowadays perfectly used to listening to *spoken prose* from a disembodied voice. Various technological advances made over the last quarter of a century have resulted in spoken language taking over many of the public, official functions that used to be the monopoly of writing. Radio news bulletins are an obvious example of this. However, although news bulletins are *spoken*, they are undoubtedly '*spoken prose*'— not 'real' spoken language, with the structure of conversation. The fact is, of course, that news bulletins *must* be read from a prepared text, and very few people can write down words which will sound, when read aloud, as if they were *not* being read but were being spontaneously produced.

4

Although we are well accustomed to hearing *spoken* prose, we are certainly not accustomed to seeing *written* conversation.[1]

If conversation is to be studied properly, it must be available in a form which is not only, as a recording is, permanent, but which is susceptible of being handled for analysis—in some visual form, in fact. We must have written texts of conversation. However, when you look at the written text of a genuine spontaneous conversation, it is pretty horrifying—particularly when it is a conversation in which you yourself have taken part. It is sometimes unintelligible, and it is always illogical, disorganized, repetitious, and ungrammatical. I have several times heard people remark, on seeing the text of a recorded conversation, that it is illiterate. But of course it *should* be illiterate—literally. It should be different from written language. We are so used to deriving our notions of what is correct and logical in language from prose, that we find it hard to realize that a quite different set of standards must be applied to conversation.

The fact is that one can't really get down a conversation in ordinary writing. Writing is a device developed for recording prose, not conversation. For instance, if you are reading aloud a piece of written prose, you infer from the text what intonations you ought to use, even if, as is almost always the case, you have a choice. The intonation, in other words, adds little information. But if you try to read aloud a piece of written conversation, you can't tell what the intonations should be—or rather what they actually were. Here the intonations contribute more independently to the meaning. To write conversation adequately, we must be able to include the intonation in the text, whereas there is no need at all to do so in writing prose.

We ought to be able to write down other things too—variations

---

[1] See Randolph Quirk in *Studies in Communication* (London, 1955), pp. 169 ff.

in tempo, in voice quality, in loudness; pauses, coughs, stammers, interjections. It is partly because these things are, necessarily, lacking in a conventionally written text of recorded conversation that it looks so foolish. A phonetic notation of a much more comprehensive kind than we possess at present is needed if we are to write down conversation with any degree of completeness.

I would like to suggest, to those who are interested, something which helps to bring this home. Try, when you are present at an informal discussion among a number of people (if possible an intellectual discussion, when people are *thinking* as they talk), withdrawing yourself from participation for a while and picturing to yourself, in your mind's eye, what the flow of words which is taking place would look like if it was written down exactly as spoken. One sees conversation in a new light by doing this; it brings out features that one had never noticed before. And one may come to realize that the more intellectual the conversation, the more curious it looks in visual form.

5

The most striking differences between spoken prose and genuine conversation are probably to be found at the phonetic level. Some of these differences are:

(1) The highly standardized intonation patterns of spoken prose as compared with those of conversation. These intonation patterns of spoken prose, for one kind of English, are very fully described in Armstrong and Ward's *A Handbook of English Intonation*, a book that hardly deals with the intonation of conversation at all.

(2) The evenness of tempo of spoken prose, compared with the frequent variations in tempo of conversation.

(3) The pauses. In spoken prose these are closely related to the grammatical structure of the sentences, but in conversation pauses seem to play a different kind of role—they frequently come at places which, in the present state of our knowledge, are unpredictable.[1] The end of a sentence, for example, is more likely to be

---

[1] More light on this problem may be expected to result from the researches of Dr Frieda Goldman-Eisler at University College, London. See, for instance, *The Quarterly Journal of Experimental Psychology*, vol. 10, 1958, pp. 96 ff.

shown by the intonation than by a pause, and pauses often come between two words in close grammatical connexion.

(4) The importance of *silence* (as distinct from pauses) in conversation. There is nothing comparable in spoken prose. Quite long stretches of silence sometimes occur in conversation between contributions of the participants. These silences seem not to be noticed at the time—at any rate they invariably cause surprise when revealed by a recording. They pass unnoticed at the time because they are filled by gestures and grimaces—the conversation continues during them, though not in words.

(5) Stammers and errors of articulation are rare in spoken prose and conspicuous when they occur; but they are the rule in conversation. What has been called 'normal non-fluency' attracts no attention. A speaker with a carefully-prepared script will sometimes, in reading it, hope to give an impromptu effect by trying to reproduce the non-fluency of conversation, but I have never heard this done convincingly.

(6) The number of phonetically different speech-sounds or 'segments' is probably far greater in conversation than in spoken prose. Phoneme theory, in its traditional form (or forms), is based on the segments of the latter, and is very much more difficult (some might say impossible) to apply to the analysis of the former.

There are, of course, many differences at other linguistic levels, as Professor Randolph Quirk has pointed out.[1] There is the *incompleteness* of conversation, or rather its apparent incompleteness: what, in prose, *must* be put into words is often in conversation perfectly clear from the context, and therefore not mentioned. Hence, in a conversational text, sentences may lack verbs, verbs may lack objects, or even subjects; and so on. The sentence as traditionally defined is really a unit of prose, not of conversation.

Repetition is another characteristic of conversation; things are frequently said several times over, sometimes in slightly varying words.

Apparently meaningless words and phrases constantly occur in conversation, for example: *sort of*; *kind of*; *you see*; *shall I say*;

---

[1] op. cit.

you know; *I mean*; *I mean to say*; *what I call*; *well*. These have been called 'intimacy signals' by Professor Quirk—they make the hearer feel at ease, and *en rapport* with the speaker. They have the function also, I think, of being *silence fillers*—they enable us to keep talking while we think of what to say next. Very common silence fillers also are *mm*, *er*, and similar noises; and repetition, too, often fulfils the same purpose.

Genuine spoken language, or 'conversation' in my sense of the term, has hardly been described at all in any language, whether from the phonetic, phonological, or grammatical point of view. How far it is possible to describe it, and how far it is worth describing, are questions which cannot be answered until more attempts have been made at doing so. But it is worth remembering that when we, as language teachers, claim we are teaching the spoken language, most of the time what we are teaching is spoken prose.

2

R.P. and local accent

The population of England consists of people who speak Standard English, and people who do not speak Standard English. And those who speak Standard English can themselves be divided into people who speak it with an accent, and people who speak it without an accent. I know these assertions are both controversial and ambiguous; and first I want to clarify them and to try to justify them, and then to show that they describe a rather unfortunate state of affairs—a kind of situation from which many other countries (perhaps all of them) are free.

First let me make clear what I mean by Standard English. This phrase is used in a variety of senses. I shall use it, as many other people do, to mean that kind of English which is the official language of the entire English-speaking world, and is also the language of all educated English-speaking people. What I mean by Standard English has nothing to do with the way people pronounce: Standard English is a language, not an accent, and it is as easily recognizable as Standard English when it is written down as when it is spoken. It is, in fact, the only form of English to be at all widely written nowadays. There is, in Standard English, a certain amount of regional variation, perhaps, but not very much—it is spoken, and even more written, with remarkable uniformity considering the area which it covers.

I ought perhaps just now to have made the distinction between those who *habitually* use Standard English and those who do not, for practically everybody these days can make a fair shot at Standard English when they want to, if they have had any schooling

Broadcast in the B.B.C. Third Programme on 29 August 1951, under the title 'Local Accent', and published in *The Listener* on 6 September 1951, under the title 'The Way People Speak'.

at all, even if they do so only occasionally. People who do not habitually use Standard English are said to use a dialect—they are dialect-speakers (though they will very seldom be dialect-writers). I have used the word dialect here to mean any form of English which differs from Standard English in grammar, syntax, vocabulary, and, of course, in pronunciation too, though a difference of pronunciation alone is not enough to make a different dialect. However, I am not concerned with dialects at the moment, only with Standard English.

Standard English, then, is a world language. I know many Americans and Scots object to it being said that they speak and write Standard *English*. But the word 'English' was apparently used of the language before it was used of a country or its inhabitants, and it seems a rather unreasonable objection. I want to talk about Standard English as spoken all over the world, and especially as spoken in England; for each country has its own type or types of pronunciation when speaking it. A South African, for example, has features of pronunciation which distinguish his Standard English from an Australian's; in the same way a Middle West American can be heard to pronounce differently from one from the Southern States.

In England there are numerous ways of pronouncing Standard English, but here the position is peculiar; there is one type of accent which is distinctively an accent of England, but is not identified with any particular part of the country. In other words, it is a regional accent when the whole English-speaking world is taken into account; but within England itself it is non-regional. This is what I meant by saying that in England some people speak Standard English with an accent, and some speak it without. Some speakers, in other words, show which part of the country they come from when they talk, and some do not. This 'accentless' pronunciation is really as much an accent as any other, and it would be convenient if it had an accepted name by which I could call it. But it has no popularly understood name, and so I shall refer to it by the initials of the phrase 'Received Pronunciation'—by the letters R.P. that is to say. This is a technical term of phoneticians.

This R.P. stands in strong contrast to all the other ways of pronouncing Standard English put together. In fact English people are divided, by the way they talk, into three groups; first, R.P. speakers of Standard English—those without an accent; second, non-R.P. speakers of Standard English—those with an accent; and third, dialect speakers. I believe this to be a situation which is not paralleled in any other country anywhere. Everywhere else the division is into speakers of the standard language, and speakers of dialect. There is usually a way of pronouncing the standard language which is more highly thought of than other ways, but it always remains a regional accent—usually that of the capital. The non-regional type of accent, which is the essence of R.P., is absent.

This state of affairs is something which is either unsuspected, or misunderstood, outside England—partly because, although English people are generally aware of the situation, they do not mention it much. As a matter of fact it is rather an embarrassing subject. It is not easy to talk about it without hurting people's feelings, because although R.P. is not the accent of a region of England, it *is* the accent of a social class, and embarrassment starts as soon as it is asked who speaks with this Received Pronunciation, and who does not.

R.P. arose, perhaps not much more than a hundred years ago, in the great public schools, and it is maintained, and transmitted from generation to generation, mainly by people educated at the public schools. There is no question of deliberately teaching it. It is picked up more or less unconsciously; and if it is not learnt in youth, it is very difficult to acquire later on in life. I think there is no equivalent to R.P. in other countries largely because the public schools are themselves unique. In spite of the fact that it has no popular name, most English people are able to identify what is meant by R.P. without any more elaborate explanations than I have given. They can recognize it when they hear it, and they have a pretty good idea whether they themselves speak it or not.

Now, we all pass judgements on other people based on the way they speak. This is true all over the world, and tiny differences in the sound of speech often provide the basis for these judgements. In fact all human beings with normal hearing have, in this sense, a good ear for language—surprising as that seems. We infer, from how people talk, where they come from, what their personalities and characters are like, what mood they are in, and so on. Similarity of accent creates immediate sympathy; difference of accent is grounds for suspicion, or at least wariness. These judgements are made unconsciously for the most part, but they have great influence on people's relationships with each other.

The existence of R.P. gives accent judgements a peculiar importance in England, and perhaps makes the English more sensitive than most people to accent differences. In England, Standard English speakers are divided by an 'accent-bar', on one side of which is R.P., and on the other side all the other accents. And very often the first judgement made on a stranger's speech is the answer to the question: which side of the accent-bar is he? Though, needless to say, the question is never formulated explicitly.

It is not easy to put into words how this accent-bar works. There is no doubt that R.P. is a privileged accent; your social life, or your career, or both, may be affected by whether you possess it or do not. Generalization, though, is difficult. Some callings attach more importance to it than others; some social circles are more linguistically exclusive than others; and there are always people of exceptional personality who are able to compensate for any type of accent. Still, I believe it is not putting it too strongly to say that in all occupations for which an educated person is required, it is an advantage to speak R.P., and it may be a disadvantage not to speak it.

Let me, before I go any further, deal briefly with one or two points which may be in your minds. It is often claimed, for example, that R.P. has intrinsic virtues: that it is the most widely intelligible spoken form of Standard English; or (less commonly) that it is the most aesthetically satisfactory of accents. That it is widely intelligible I would not deny; though its aesthetic merits are more dubious. But in any case these claims are difficult to uphold simply because, considered objectively as sound, the differences between R.P. and some of the regional accents are very small: so small that they may not be apparent except to the English—a foreigner, for instance, who knows English well may often fail to spot them. If the differences are as small as that, they can hardly be important aesthetically or for intelligibility.

Although it is fair for us in England to describe R.P. as accentless English, that is, English without regional indications, it must be remembered that it is not so for the rest of the English-speaking world. Outside England, it seems to have no special prestige, and it appears just as regional to an American, say, as any other way of pronouncing English. Conversely, there are other accents which rank socially equal, in England, with R.P.—but these are never accents of England. Most forms of Irish, Scots, American, Canadian, for example, or any foreign accent, are acceptable.

It might seem at first a good thing that there is something that can be described as an accentless form of English; and it has been suggested that R.P. should be taught to everybody in the country, and so made a national standard in England. Some educationists in Scotland and America have even proposed that it should be made a standard for those countries, too. I doubt if it would be possible to teach it in the schools. But even if, at the cost of a great deal of teaching time, it could be done, do we really want a standard pronunciation? Other countries do not have one: they are content with a number of regional accents sufficiently similar to be mutually intelligible. The existence of a standard pronunciation such as R.P. is, I suggest, a bad rather than a good thing. It is an anachronism in present-day democratic society. There was a time when R.P. provided a safe clue to certain things about a speaker—his suitability for certain types of job, or (for other R.P. speakers) the congeniality of his company. It indicated being accustomed to authority; a liberal education; interest in, or at least some knowledge of, the arts: for those who spoke R.P. in those days had practically a monopoly of those virtues. They have no longer such a monopoly. But many people react to an absence of R.P. as if it necessarily accompanied an absence of other things also—of those accomplishments which are nowadays the common property of everyone in England who speaks Standard English. This was pointed out in the House of Commons a few years ago, during a discussion on commissions in the services, by a speaker who said that the phrase 'officer-like qualities and the power of command' means nothing more than the right kind of accent. And I have several times come across people who were unable to bring themselves to take seriously a radio talk on a serious subject if it was not delivered in R.P. In short, it is misleading to call R.P. the accent of educated people, as is often done. For although those who talk R.P. can justly consider themselves educated, they are outnumbered these days by the undoubtedly educated people who do not talk R.P.

All over the world people are intolerant of each other's accents: unfamiliar customs seem as silly and wrong in speech as they do in everything else. But the exceptional accent-bar of England gives this natural human intolerance an exceptional importance. I believe that the continued existence of this accent-bar, which no longer reflects social reality, is having a harmful effect on Standard English speech in England. As a consequence of it more and more people who are well educated, but have not had an opportunity to learn R.P., are made nervous and anxious about their speech-sounds. Lack of confidence in one's accent focuses attention on the mechanics of talking, which should be automatic. Preoccupation with how one is speaking can upset the whole of one's delivery, produce unpleasant voice-quality, destroy self-confidence, even perhaps interfere with thinking.

Many people, I know, feel a vague disquiet at this situation, but it is all very well just to ask for tolerance. The accent-bar is a little like a colour-bar—to many people, on the right side of the bar, it appears eminently reasonable. It is very difficult to believe, if you talk R.P. yourself, that it is not intrinsically superior to other accents. Until all regional educated accents are genuinely felt in England to be socially equal with R.P., these consequences of the accent-bar will persist. I have tried to draw attention to the problem rather than to suggest a solution. It is a problem which is getting more pressing, and some day a solution will have to be found.

3

A phonetician's view of verse structure

May I say, right away, that my interest in prosody, in the study of verse structure, is not an *amateur's* interest. I would like to claim prosody as part of my own subject, phonetics; and I would therefore assert that my interest in prosody is a professional one.

It is true that, in fact, most phoneticians have paid little attention to verse structure. Most writers on prosody, moreover, have paid little attention to phonetics, which is possibly why they have never reached any agreement on a common body of knowledge.

I claim prosody as part of my subject, because verse *is* verse as a result of the way certain aspects of the sound, or rather perhaps the sound-producing movements, of speech have been exploited or organized. The study of the sound of speech, in all its aspects, and of the bodily movements which produce the sound, is the province of phonetics. Phonetic techniques of observation and analysis can be applied to verse structure as successfully as they can to any other aspect of language where the sound is important. I would like to start, therefore, with that part of elementary phonetic theory which is relevant to our present purpose.

Speech, as is well known, depends on breathing: the sounds of speech are produced by an *air-stream* from the lungs. This air-stream does not issue from the lungs in a continuous flow, as might be thought at first. The flow is 'pulse-like': there is a continuous and rapid fluctuation in the air-pressure, which results from alternate contractions and relaxations of the breathing muscles. Each muscular contraction, and consequent rise in

Paper given to the Durham English Society in May 1961, and published in *Linguistics*, No. 6, 1964.

air-pressure, is a *chest-pulse* (so called because it is the intercostal muscles in the chest that are responsible); and each chest-pulse constitutes a syllable. This syllable-producing process, the system of chest-pulses, is the basis of human speech.[1]

This, however, is not the whole story of the production of the air-stream which we use for talking; there is in addition a second system of pulse-like muscular movements on which in part it depends. This system consists of a series of less frequent, more powerful contractions of the breathing muscles which every now and then coincide with, and reinforce, a chest-pulse, and cause a more considerable and more sudden rise in air-pressure. These reinforcing movements constitute the system of *stress-pulses*, and this system is combined in speech with the system of chest-pulses.

The rhythm of speech is a rhythm of these two systems of pulses: it is a product of the way they are combined in producing an air-stream for talking. The rhythm is already *in* the air-stream, in fact, before the actual vowels and consonants which make up words are superimposed on it.

The two pulse systems are, as far as we know, present when all languages are being spoken, but languages co-ordinate them in different ways. Two different kinds of periodicity can result from their organization: the pulses in either the one, or the other, of the two systems can be made to recur at equal intervals of time. *Either* the stress-producing pulses *or* the syllable-producing pulses can be in isochronous sequence, and in the former case we have a *stress-timed* rhythm, in the latter a *syllable-timed* rhythm (to use terms which have recently become widely current).[2] The languages of the world fall into two classes, depending on whether the rhythm with which they are spoken is stress-timed or syllable-timed. English is a typical example of a language with a stress-timed rhythm. French is a typical example of a language with a syllable-timed one.

It may not be immediately obvious that a necessary consequence of having one series of pulses in isochronous sequence is that the

---

[1] For further details see R. H. Stetson, *Motor Phonetics* (Amsterdam, 1951).

[2] They were put forward by K. L. Pike, *The Intonation of American English* (Ann Arbor, 1946).

other series *cannot* be in isochronous sequence; but it is so. Thus if, as in English, the isochronous pulses are the stress-pulses, it follows that the chest-pulses will come at unequal intervals of time. An illustration may help to make clear why this must be the case.

Let us consider the utterance:

This is the house that Jack built.

It contained, as I spoke it then, four stress-pulses, and they occurred on the syllables *This*, *house*, *Jack* and *built*. Now if I say the sentence again, and while I do so tap with a pencil on the table every time there is a stress-pulse, the taps will be unmistakably isochronous, showing that the stressed syllables are too. But there are seven syllables in all in the sentence. Suppose I now tap on *every* syllable: it is at once plain that *they* are *not* isochronous —they are unevenly spaced in time. A moment's thought shows why: the unstressed syllables are unequally distributed between the stressed ones, and must therefore be spoken at varying speeds to fill the spaces between the latter, being sometimes compressed and sometimes expanded and therefore constantly varying in rate of succession. (We recognize, incidentally, as a typical French mispronunciation the use of isochronous chest-pulses in this sentence.)

The stress-timed rhythm of English is the basis of the structure of English verse, and syllable-timed rhythm need claim our attention no further.

The rhythmic basis of verse is thus the same as that of prose (and, it should be added, of conversation too)—as far, at any rate, as English is concerned. I shall say later what I consider to be the crucial difference between prose and verse; but I do not believe their rhythmic features to be different *in kind* from each other. In fact any smallish sequence of words taken out of verse *could* be a bit of conversation, and any smallish excerpt from conversation *could* be a bit of verse. This explains why poets have no need of prosodic theory in order to compose verse, and why listeners and readers, equally, have no need of special knowledge in order to appreciate verse: all that they need is already there, in their normal experience of the language.

I said, at the beginning, that it was rather the *sound-producing movements*, than the sound of speech itself, of which the organization in a special way results in verse. All rhythm, it seems likely, is ultimately rhythm of bodily movement. Language rhythm is thus something which belongs primarily to the *speaker*, rather than the hearer; something which arises out of the speaker's movements, and especially out of the muscular movements which produce the air-stream. It is natural to ask, therefore, how it is that rhythm can exist for the *hearer*.

The explanation, briefly, is that our perception of speech—not only its rhythmic side, but other features of it too—depends to a considerable extent on the hearer identifying himself with the speaker. As we listen to the sounds of speech, we perceive them not simply as sounds, but as clues to movements. It is an intuitive reaction of the hearer to be aware of the movements of the various organs of speech which the speaker is making. We perceive speech in muscular terms. This is perhaps part of what I. A. Richards meant when he said that metre 'is not *in* the stimulation, it is in our response'.[1]

It has been pointed out that a somewhat analogous situation may obtain in listening to music. As P. E. Vernon has written, 'rhythm is an aspect of music that is more of a bodily than an auditory nature', and he points out that many people perceive music in terms of their hands at the piano or other instruments.[2] This is probably to some extent true of every musical performer when listening to others; but we are all, when it comes to language, performers.

Speech rhythm, and therefore the rhythm of verse, is *in* the speaker, and it is in the hearer in so far as he identifies himself with the speaker. We might coin the term 'phonetic empathy' for the process by which he does so. In order to be able to 'empathize', of course, the hearer must know a language intimately; probably it is necessary for it to be his mother tongue, in most cases.

The rhythm of speech, therefore, is primarily muscular rhythm, a rhythm of bodily movement, rather than a rhythm of sound.

[1] *Principles of Literary Criticism* (London, 1924), p. 139.
[2] In *The Pleasures of Music*, ed. Jacques Barzun (London, 1952), p. 173.

This is why verse can be immediately recognized and felt as verse in *silent* reading, which otherwise would not be easy to explain.

I must next make an important point: that a stress pulse can occur without sound accompanying it. There is one famous and often quoted example of this; attention was drawn to it first, I think, by Daniel Jones.[1] The phrase *thank you*, when spoken in a perfunctory way, is often pronounced in England in a way that can be represented in phonetic transcription as [ˈk̩kju]. As far as the ear is concerned, the first syllable has disappeared; as most people say the phrase, however, it is still present in the speaker's movements—and present, moreover, as a stressed syllable.

In this instance, although there is silence in the place of the initial stressed syllable, the speaker makes a movement of the articulators as well as of the breathing muscles: he actually says a long [k] at the beginning of the word. But a stress-pulse may also occur in English at a point during an utterance where there is a gap in the sequence of words, and there is no articulatory movement. This is what happens when I say something like the following: 'A funny thing happened to me, on my way here this evening.' Between 'me' and 'on', as I said the sentence then, there is what may be called a *silent stress-pulse*, as distinct from an actual *stressed syllable* (which would be a stress with some articulatory movements superimposed on it). We can say, therefore, that that utterance contained six stress-pulses, one of which was silent and the other five were stressed syllables (*fun*ny, *hap*pened, *me*, *way*, *eve*ning).

Such silent stresses are not a matter of chance, nor of the speaker's whim, and they merit more linguistic investigation than they have received so far. When one starts listening for them they turn out to be surprisingly frequent in conversation, and even more frequent in prose read aloud. Moreover, as we shall see, they are an integral part of the structure of English verse.

From now on, therefore, I shall use the word 'stress', by itself, to mean simply the rhythmical recurrence of the reinforced chest

---

[1] *Outline of English Phonetics* (Cambridge, 1932), p. 227.

pulse; it may coincide with an articulated syllable, which will then be a stressed syllable; or it may be a silent stress.

One must not suppose that because a silent stress *is* silent, it therefore does not exist for the hearer. There is a *stress*, even if not a stressed syllable; and this stress is felt by the speaker and (because he would do the same if he were speaking) 'empathized' by the hearer.

I should now like to be historical for a moment. The strongest influence on prosodic speculation in England has, of course, been classical prosody, the theory of the structure of Latin verse and, originally, of Greek verse. Most writers on the subject until the end of the eighteenth century believed that the principles and categories of analysis of Latin verse could be applied to English verse; or at least that they could be adapted so that they would apply. It was even believed by some that if they couldn't be adapted, then English verse should be written in such a way that they *would* fit. Latin verse was based on syllable quantity. All attempts to apply this basis to English failed. Since the appearance of Coleridge's preface to *Christabel*, however, in 1816, theories of prosody have been largely transformed.[1]

What Coleridge said in his preface was, 'The metre of "Christabel" is . . . founded on a new principle: namely, that of counting in each line the accents, not the syllables'; and he goes on to say, 'In each line the accents will be found to be only four.'

This has often been taken to mean, both by Coleridge's followers and by his opponents, that English verse is regulated by the number of stressed (or accented) syllables in the line. However, if the 'new principle' is formulated in this way, it will not really work. *Christabel* itself, it is true, usually has four stressed syllables in the line:

Tis the 'middle of 'night by the 'castle 'clock

(I show the stressed syllables in the usual manner by the stress-mark ' at the beginning of the syllable.) Sometimes, however, there seem to be only three stressed syllables:

My 'sire is of a 'noble 'line.

[1] T. S. Omond, *English Metrists* (Oxford, 1921), Ch. IV.

The formulation of the 'new principle' should, of course, be to the effect that a line such as one of *Christabel* contains four *stress-pulses*, not stressed *syllables* (and it is perhaps possible to interpret Coleridge in this sense). In other words, we must be prepared for some of the stresses to be silent. In the line quoted immediately above, for instance, a silent stress comes between 'sire' and 'is': the line contains three stressed syllables, but four stress-pulses, one of which, though silent, is nevertheless as much sensuously present as the others.

If we look for five stressed syllables in English blank verse, we will often fail to find them. But nearly always, when we so fail, we *can* find—usually we cannot avoid finding—five *stresses*, some of which may fall on silence. To quote two famous instances (the caret, $_\wedge$, may be conveniently used to indicate any silence or pause which forms an integral part of the structure of a line; '$_\wedge$ therefore indicates a silent stress):

> To 'be or 'not to be, '$_\wedge$ 'that is the 'question
> Of 'man's 'first diso'bedience, '$_\wedge$ and the 'fruit[1]

The recurrent stress pulses in a line of English verse give rise to units which we may call (following many others) *feet*. A foot, in this usage, may be defined as the space in time from the incidence of one stress-pulse up to, but not including, the next stress-pulse. Thus, with this definition, it is the same thing to say that a given line consists of a certain number of feet as that it contains a certain number of stresses, and I shall prefer to put it in the former way from now on. If we use the conventional vertical line to indicate the limits of the foot we can dispense with the stress mark:

> 'Tis the | middle of | night by the | castle | clock |
> My | sire | $_\wedge$ is of a | noble | line |
> To | be or | not to be | $_\wedge$ | that is the | question |
> Of | man's | first diso|bedience, | $_\wedge$ and the | fruit |

English verse, it is clear, like classical verse, depends on a rhythm which is temporally organized—it depends on the division of time into temporal units. English verse must be therefore in some sense

---

[1] These two scansions were put forward by Joshua Steele (see Ch. IV).

quantitative. As in Latin verse, all the feet within a piece of English verse are of equal length or quantity.

(It is of interest that the foot, defined as above, turns out to be of importance in several other ways in the study of English.)

There remain three points to be dealt with in order to complete this very brief phonetician's outline of the structure of English verse.

The first point is that silent stresses are much more frequent than one at first would suppose. Several writers have at different times put forward the theory that all lines of English verse contain an *even* number of feet. Where it seems at first that a line contains an odd number, there is always a silent final stress at the end of the line which brings the number of feet up to an even one. Thus lines which are commonly supposed to have, for instance, three, or five, feet really have four, or six. The so-called 'iambic penta-meter', therefore, goes like this:

| Know then thy|self, pre|sume not | God to | scan | ∧ |

—the silent final stress forming the beginning of the sixth foot must be inserted before the next line can be started. And the limerick, which is a verse-form reputed to begin with two three-foot lines, really goes like this:

There | was an old | man in a | tree | ∧
Who was | horribly | bored by a | bee | ∧
When they | said, does it | buzz,
He rep|lied, yes it | does,
It's a | regular | brute of a | bee. | ∧ |

(The unstressed syllables which begin each line are attached to the silent stress concluding the preceding line, forming with it a 'line-divided' foot—except for the anacrusis which begins the stanza.) This theory is, then, to the effect that the *double* foot, or 'dipode', is the measure of verse in English. It certainly seems to be true in a very large number of cases, whether or not it applies without exception to the whole corpus of English verse.

The second point concerns the variety of the feet themselves, which is considerable: we find in English verse many more kinds of feet than in Latin verse, for example. This variety is of two kinds:

it lies both in the number of syllables, and in the relative length
or quantity of the syllables, which are in the foot. The number
of syllables may vary from none (if it is a completely silent foot)
to four or even occasionally more. In

| Know then thy|self, pre|sume not | God to | scan |

there is one three-syllable foot, three of two syllables, and one
one-syllable foot. The relative length of syllables is a further
source of variety, even between feet containing the same number
of syllables. Syllable-quantity, in other words, is a factor which
cannot really be left out of account (though it usually is) in
examining the structure of English verse. When a foot consists
of two syllables, for example, it does not necessarily follow that
these syllables will divide the time of the foot into two equal
halves. They may do so; but they may divide it into (approximately) one-third and two-thirds respectively, or conversely into
two-thirds and one-third. Take the line from Milton's *L'Allegro*:

| Meadows | trim with | daisies | pide

It contains three two-syllable feet, but they are manifestly different
from each other in their syllable quantities. In |meadows| the
first syllable is shorter than the second; in |trim with| the first
syllable is longer than the second; and in |daisies| the two syllables
are of equal length (this is true, at least, of my pronunciation).
These quantities, it must be emphasized, are not haphazard, but
follow strict rules, which, however, there is no time on this occasion
to expound.[1] Three-syllable and four-syllable feet offer even
greater possibilities of variation. It should be remembered that
syllable-quantity in English is entirely distinct from stress: the
two factors are quite independent of each other. Syllable quantity
must not, moreover, be confused with vowel quantity; a so-called
'short' vowel often occurs in a long syllable (as in *trim* above).

The third point concerns the line itself. The foot, and the
syllable quantities within the foot, are phonological categories
which are just as much needed to describe English prose or
conversation as they are to describe verse; but the line is a unit

---

[1] See the following chapter.

of rhythm which occurs in verse only. Prose is rhythmic but not metrical (as Aristotle said), but verse is both rhythmic and metrical. The rhythmic unit of both prose and verse is the foot; the metrical unit of verse is the line. This is the crucial difference between the two modes: in prose the feet are not organized into a higher metrical unit.

A line of verse, if it is to function as a unit, must of course be recognizable to the ear as such—it must be delimited. This is done by various devices which may be called *line-end markers*, and there seem to be three of these in use in modern English verse. All three may be used together, or any two, or any one alone. They are:

(a) rhyme, or assonance,
(b) a silent final stress,
(c) a monosyllabic foot, not used anywhere else, concluding the words of the line.

All three of these line-end markers can be seen operating in Gray's *Elegy*:

The | curfew | tolls the | knell of | parting | day, | ∧
The | lowing | herd wind | slowly | o'er the | lea, | ∧
The | plowman | homeward | plods his | weary | way, | ∧
And | leaves the | world to | darkness | ∧ and to | me. | ∧ |

English verse thus turns out, as Hopkins suggested it would, to be really rather simple in its structure. The complicated thing that has sometimes been made of it is due partly, I think, to the lingering influence of classical prosody; and partly to lack of knowledge of the elementary phonetic facts that lie behind all speech rhythm.

3

4

Syllable quantity and enclitics in English

It is a necessary consequence of the fact that English is a language which is spoken with a stress-timed rhythm[1] that its syllables are of uneven length. It is usually held, though, that there is nothing systematic about the way that the length of its syllables varies, and that there are no laws to be discovered behind the variation. As Catherine Ing says, 'English syllables have not in natural speech any consistent relations to each other in quantity.'[2] The present paper is tentative, and deliberately skirts round a number of problems, but it expresses the belief that there *are* consistent relations of quantity to be found between English syllables, and that these relations are quite important in the phonetics and phonology of English.

In spite of the widely-held conviction that English syllable-quantity cannot be systematized, a number of writers have at times, and for various reasons, given fairly precise indications of

---

[1] The earliest person I know to draw attention to this fact is Joshua Steele in *An Essay towards Establishing the Melody and Measure of Speech*, London, 1775 (see the following chapter). Among later writers, Coventry Patmore is noteworthy: 'A simple series of isochronous intervals, marked by accents, is as natural to spoken language as an even pace is to walking' ('English Metrical Critics', *The North British Review*, XXVII, 1857, 127-61). The convenient terms 'syllable-timed' and 'stress-timed' for what Lloyd James (in *Speech Signals in Telephony*, London, 1940, 25) called 'machine-gun rhythm' and 'morse-code rhythm' are due to K. L. Pike (see *The Intonation of American English*, Ann Arbor, 1946, 35).
[2] *Elizabethan Lyrics*, London, 1952, 195. She falls into the common error, when arguing this view, of equating syllable quantity with vowel quantity.

Paper given at the meeting of the Linguistics Association (Great Britain) at Hull in May 1961, and published in *In Honour of Daniel Jones*, London (Longmans), 1964.

relative syllable lengths, usually by means of musical notation. Daniel Jones, for instance, has shown certain syllable quantities in his *Outline of English Phonetics* from the first edition onwards.[1] Other writers who have done the same include D. S. MacColl, William Thomson, M. W. Croll, E. A. Sonnenschein, Thomas Taig, A. Classe, N. C. Scott, W. Jassem, W. S. Allen.[2] There is on the whole a remarkable degree of agreement among these writers in the quantities they allot to syllables (though they are not, for the most part, acquainted with each other's works). Most of them, however, make no attempt to work out the factors which determine the quantities, or to classify the patterns they form. Sonnenschein tried to formulate rules from which the quantity of any given syllable could be predicted, but although complex they do not account for many of the quantities he himself adduces. Daniel Jones[3] is an exception, however, and his rather brief discussion of the factors concerned has been well summarized by André Classe.[4] Jones's observations formed the starting point of my investigations, which will, I hope, themselves provide a basis for further research.

The main difficulty in the way of investigation always seems to have been the assumption that if rules are to be found for syllable quantity in English, they must be similar to the rules for syllable quantity in a language such as, say, Latin. In Latin (we are led to believe) the quantity of a syllable is a product of its

---

[1] See p. 109 of the first edition (Leipzig, 1918: mostly in print by 1914). In later editions Jones rather guardedly says that the quantities shown 'are not the lengths of the syllables but the lengths separating the "stress-points" or "peaks of prominence" of the syllables'.

[2] D. S. MacColl, 'Rhythm in English Verse, Prose, and Speech', *Essays and Studies*, v, Oxford, 1914; William Thomson, *The Rhythm of Speech*, Glasgow, 1923; M. W. Croll, *The Rhythm of English Verse*, Princeton, 1925; E. A. Sonnenschein, *What is Rhythm?*, Oxford, 1925; Thomas Taig, *Rhythm and Metre*, Cardiff, 1929; A. Classe, *The Rhythm of English Prose*, Oxford, 1939; N. C. Scott, 'Distinctive Rhythm', *Le Maître Phonétique*, 1940, 6; W. Jassem, *Intonation of Conversational English*, Wroclaw, 1952, 41; W. S. Allen, *Living English Speech*, London, 1954.

[3] *Outline of English Phonetics*, 3rd ed., Cambridge, 1932.

[4] *The Rhythm of English Prose*, 102.

phonematic structure, and all syllables of the same phonematic structure have the same quantity wherever they occur in the word or the utterance. This is not true of English, however, where, as Jones recognized, the same phonematic structure is by no means always accompanied by the same syllable quantity. Clearly, the factors are not so simple in English; in fact the phonematic structure of the syllable is of small importance, and may at times be quite irrelevant.

We need first, in English, to establish a unit within which, rhythmically, the syllable functions. I shall call this unit the *foot*, using the word as many, though certainly not all, writers on English prosody have. English utterances may be considered as being divided by the isochronous beat of the stress pulse into feet of (approximately) even length. Each foot starts with a stress and contains everything that follows that stress up to, but not including, the next stress. '*This is the* '*house that* '*Jack* '*built* has therefore four feet, and they can be most conveniently indicated by the use of vertical lines:

|This is the|house that|Jack|built|

The quantity of any syllable is a proportion of the total length of the foot within which the syllable occurs, and it is relative to the quantity of any other syllable in the foot. We cannot therefore say anything about the quantity of a syllable until we know its place in the foot.

Perhaps at this point a reminder should be issued, to prevent possible misunderstandings, that (1) syllable quantity is not directly dependent on either (a) vowel quantity or (b) stress; (2) the foot is independent of word boundaries.

It is clear that, since feet are of even length, as they must be if delimited by the isochronous stress pulse, the number of syllables in a given foot will have a direct effect on their length. In a monosyllabic foot the quantity of the syllable and the quantity of the foot coincide; here phonematic structure is totally irrelevant. In

|four|large|black|dogs|

every syllable has the same quantity, though their phonematic structures are very different. In a disyllabic foot it is obvious that neither syllable can be as long as the syllable in a mono-syllabic foot; and in a trisyllabic foot some at least of the syllables must of necessity be shorter than those of a disyllabic foot. The number of syllables in the foot is, however, not the only thing which must be taken into account when establishing the quantity of a syllable. The often-quoted minimal pair of sentences produced by Scott[1]

> take Grey to London
> take Greater London

shows how two disyllabic feet, |*Grey to*| and |*Greater*|, having, moreover, the same phonematic structure /greitə/, may be composed of clearly different syllable quantities. An examination of types of disyllabic feet will provide the simplest illustration of the principles underlying syllable quantity in English (as exemplified in my own pronunciation).

For the purposes of analysis it is convenient to regard disyllabic feet as being in *triple* time; that is to say a foot is to be looked on as containing three units of time, between which the syllables are divided (as compared with *duple* or common time, when the foot contains two or four units of time). This is probably no more than a convenience, largely of notation. (I believe it to be characteristic of prose and conversation that one cannot tell whether the time is duple or triple—it is constantly ambiguous in this respect; whereas the time of verse is usually clearly heard to be either the one or the other, even though occasionally it may be necessary to wait a line or two after the beginning of a poem before being sure.)

There are three types of disyllabic foot. The first, which we may call Type A, has a short syllable followed by a long syllable, that is to say, in musical notation, ♩ ♩, or 1 time-unit followed by 2 time-units. Examples are |*shilling*|, |*never*|, |*atom*|, |*cuckoo*|. I shall represent the syllable quantities of this foot as ∪ —, making use of the symbols of traditional metrical notation, in spite of their misuse these days, and intending that they should

---

[1] 'Distinctive Rhythm', *Le Maître Phonétique*, 1940, 6.

be taken literally. A convenient name for it is a 'short-long' foot (it is a pity we cannot call it an 'iamb', which, in the original sense of that word, it is; but it would probably be too confusing).

Many people find the syllable quantities of feet of this type difficult to hear at first, though their existence has often been pointed out (see, e.g. Sweet[1] and many of the writers quoted above in the second paragraph). There is often felt to be something anomalous in a syllable which is stressed and yet short, followed by an unstressed one which is long. Sweet considered (see Sonnenschein[2]) that this relation of quantities goes back a long way in English, and accounts for the retention of the final *u* in O E *scipu* as compared with its loss in *hus* or *word*. My impression is that nowadays there are some types of English where Type A is not found.

The second type of disyllabic foot, Type B, contains two syllables of equal length, ♩ ♩ , or $1\frac{1}{2}$ time-units followed by $1\frac{1}{2}$ time-units. Examples are |*greater*|, |*firmly*|, |*centre*|, de|*cisive*|, |*matches*|. The traditional metrical notation does not provide us with a symbol for this syllable quantity, but a satisfactory one can easily be invented by turning the 'short' symbol upside-down, ∩. The foot can thus be represented as ∩ ∩. It is convenient to call this an 'equal-equal' foot (we could not really call it a spondee, even if the term was not spoilt, since a spondee is essentially a foot in duple time).

These two types of feet, therefore, give us three different syllable quantities:

∪	short	♩	1 time-unit
∩	medium	♩.	$1\frac{1}{2}$ time-units
—	long	♩	2 time-units

It is clear, also, that a third type of foot is possible, which we can call Type C, 'long-short', or ♩ ♩ . Examples are |*Grey to*|, |*tea for*| two, I'll|see you a|*gain to*|morrow, per|*haps I*| did. (We had better not call this a 'trochee', for the same reason that 'iamb' is best avoided.)

[1] H. Sweet, *A New English Grammar*, Oxford, 1892, 300.
[2] *What is Rhythm?*, 136.

The three types of disyllabic foot, therefore, are:

$$A \cup -$$
$$B \cap \cap$$
$$C - \cup$$

We must now consider the factors on which syllable quantities in a disyllabic foot depend. Type C is the simplest case: the quantities $- \cup$ depend on the presence of a *word-boundary* within the foot, as can be inferred from the examples given above. In this type of disyllabic foot, therefore, the phonematic structure of the syllables plays no part in determining their quantity. (We shall see below that, while the quantities of a Type C foot always imply a word-division between the two syllables, there are certain conditions under which such a word-division does not imply Type C quantities.)

A foot of the two remaining types, Type A and Type B, must consist either of a two-syllable word with the stress on the first syllable, or of the last two syllables of a penultimately-stressed longer word. In these cases the syllable quantities depend on phonematic structure. Three possible phonematic structures of the foot are concerned, and they may be represented in the following formulae, in which C = any consonant; (C) means that the presence or absence of a consonant is immaterial; V = any vowel or diphthong, or a syllabic liquid; V^1 = the so-called 'short' vowels (i.e. in the traditional Jones numbering, numbers 2, 3, 4, 6, 8, 10); V^2 = the so-called 'long' vowels and the diphthongs (numbers 1, 5, 7, 9, 11, and 13-21):

(i) $(C)V^1CV(C)$

(ii) $(C)VCC(C)V(C)$

(iii) $(C)V^2(C)V(C)$

Examples of structure (i), which produces a foot of Type A, are *meadow*, *record*, *silly*, together with the other examples of Type A given above. Examples of structure (ii) are *limpid*, *fainting*, *youngster*, and examples of structure (iii) are *drawing*, *open*, *orchard*; both structures produce a foot of Type B, and further examples of both have been given above.

There is a greater variety of syllable-quantity patterns in trisyllabic feet. The syllable quantities can clearly be heard to be different in, for example, each of the following feet:

|one for the| road
|anything| more
|seven o'|clock
|after the| war
|nobody| knows

The factors which govern these quantities are of the same sort as in the case of disyllabic feet; but there is no need to discuss in detail how they apply. Here too word-division plays an important part, and it does in still longer feet also.

There are times, however, when the presence of a word-boundary within a foot does not produce the syllable quantities expected. |Stop her|, for example, is Type A (as Sweet on more than one occasion pointed out), and |take it| is Type B: that is to say, the phonematic structure in both of these examples has determined the syllabic quantities, just as if there was no word-boundary. Her and it, in other words, are enclitics, in these particular feet.

The most frequent occasions on which such enclitics are found occur when a verb is immediately followed within a foot by a pronoun of any kind, whether object, as in the two preceding examples, or subject, as in |did he|, or indirect object, as in |tell him|. There seems to be invariably enclitic in |is there|, |may there|, and similar constructions. Of is sometimes enclitic, as for example in |piece of |, but the conditions under which this happens are not entirely clear. It is of interest that enclitics may be revealed by factors other than rhythmic ones; for instance in | feel it|, where it is enclitic and the foot is Type B, the [l] is a 'clear' one as in feeling, and clearly distinguished from the [l] in: (I may not look ill but I) | feel ill|.

I was led to investigate the problem of syllable quantity as a result of having to lecture to foreign students of English on the structure of verse, and having, because of their mistakes in reading verse, to examine it somewhat more closely than would have been necessary with native English speakers. It now seems to me impossible to give an adequate account of English prosody for any purpose without taking syllable quantities into account— since the rhythm of verse is a rhythm in time. Syllable quantity is of interest in other connexions too, however, and a consideration of it may help to throw light on disputed points. It is worth noting, for example, that in my pronunciation *matches* [matʃiz], *fetches* [fetʃiz] are feet of Type B, i.e. for me [tʃ] functions as CC and not C, so that the syllables are of structure (ii) above, and not (i); and the same applies to [dʒ]. (I have observed, moreover, that for a number of people the vowel [a] is V^2 and not V^1, as shown by the syllable quantities of the feet in which it occurs.)

The difference between V^1 and V^2 in a monosyllabic foot of the structure (C)VC is, as is well known, a difference which manifests itself over almost the whole word, being apparent in the length of C as much as in the length of V: compare *slip* and *sleep*. It is not so often pointed out that in *slipper*: *sleeper* the difference here too manifests itself over most of the word: it is true that the first vowel in *slipper* is shorter than the first in *sleeper*, but the second vowel in *slipper* is longer than the second in *sleeper* (at least in my pronunciation and that of others who speak like me). The use of the terms 'short vowel' and 'long vowel' for V^1 and V^2 is thus to some extent misleading, and it is better to think of V^1 as producing, when in the first syllable of a structure (C)VCV(C), the quantities ∪ —, and of V^2 as producing, in the same structure, the quantities ∩ ∩.

I have found it worth while drawing the attention of foreign learners of English to this point, the common mispronunciation of e.g. *ceasing* as — ∪ being often due to no more than taking 'long' as opposed to 'short' vowel too literally (a misunderstanding which may be reinforced by transcription). More serious rhythmic difficulties, of course, arise for many learners of English. Speakers of syllable-timed languages inevitably have trouble in establishing the foot as a unit in their speech. Speakers of stress-timed languages too have their difficulties, though the foot itself is not a problem. Many Scandinavian learners, for example, consistently use (following the patterns of their mother tongue) Type B feet instead of Type A. Such a mistake is perhaps not very serious as far as intelligibility goes; more troublesome is the common use by German speakers of Type C feet instead of Type B, which misleads the listener into thinking a word-division is present. Difficulties of this sort seem more easily discussed in terms of syllable quantities than segment quantities.

Finally, one might mention that considerable variation is found in syllable-quantity patterns among the various accents of Standard English, and in English dialects. In Yorkshire, for instance, a word such as *Peter* is said with the quantities — ∪, while the same word in Lowland Scots has the quantities ∪ —. It may be that the R.P. pattern for this and other similar words, ∩ ∩, is one of the most characteristic things about R.P.

5

Steele, Monboddo and Garrick

James Boswell tells us, in his *Life of Dr Johnson*, how inadequate he feels the printed word to be for conveying the full flavour of Dr Johnson's talk. 'I cannot too frequently request of my readers', he wrote, 'while they peruse my account of Johnson's conversation, to endeavour to keep in mind his deliberate and strong utterance. His mode of speaking was indeed very impressive; and I wish it could be preserved as musick is written, according to the very ingenious method of Mr Steele, who has shewn how the recitation of Mr Garrick, and other eminent speakers, might be transmitted to posterity.'

The 'ingenious method' of this Mr Steele, and his notes on Garrick's recitation, were made public in a beautifully produced book called *An Essay towards Establishing the Melody and Measure of Speech, to be Expressed and Perpetuated by Peculiar Symbols*, which was published in London in the year 1775. It was his only book, and it was re-issued four years later—the year of Garrick's death— with a new title-page and the shorter title *Prosodia Rationalis*, and with the addition of some forty more pages of comments from, and replies to, various critics.[1] It is a pity that Boswell did not learn Steele's notation, for Johnson lived another nine years after it was made public. It would not have been easy for Boswell to learn (as far as I know, the notation has never been used in its full form by anyone but its author); but it would have given us some indication, rough perhaps but fascinating, of what Johnson

---

[1] Joshua Steele, F.R.S., was born in 1700 and died, on his estates in Barbados, in 1791.

Broadcast in the B.B.C. Third Programme on 9 March 1951, under the title 'How Garrick Spoke Shakespeare'. Footnotes have been added and a few changes made in the text as broadcast.

actually sounded like. Although it needed a keenly analytic ear, such as Steele himself must have possessed, to be able to write the notation, it is not really very difficult to interpret; and later on I want to demonstrate what the all-too-brief transcription which the book contains of David Garrick reciting Hamlet's soliloquy sounds like.[1] But first it is necessary to say something about what exactly Steele meant by 'the melody and measure' of speech, and what sort of a notation his 'peculiar symbols' provided.

The letters in which language is normally written do not represent more than a part of spoken language. Writing, of course, is perfectly intelligible without these missing ingredients. But then writing is a medium for language in its own right, and though it is, in the last analysis, constructed on the basis of spoken language, the aim of writing is not, usually, to represent actual spoken utterances which have occurred. But if we should want to get down on paper the precise way in which a particular person said a particular thing, then it is at once clear that ordinary writing, as Boswell complained, will leave all-important features out. This elusive side of spoken language was first set down in a clear and systematic visual form—was first given symbols *peculiar* to itself—by Joshua Steele.

The things missing from ordinary writing are first what Steele called *melody*, and second, *measure*. Melody is nowadays called *intonation*, in the technical language of phoneticians. It is not, oddly enough, a matter of common knowledge that the voice is continually rising and falling, along established patterns, the whole time we are talking. These patterns or tunes constitute the intonation; but most people are not consciously aware of them, and some find difficulty in perceiving them when their attention is first drawn to them. Steele's purpose in publishing his book, though he had 'long nourished the matter of it in private' he said (he was seventy-five years old when he published it), was to refute another writer who had shown himself insensitive to

---

[1] The transcription was read aloud, at the end of the broadcast, by Mr J. C. Catford.

intonation. This other writer was the eccentric and learned Scottish judge, Lord Monboddo.[1] Monboddo was an acute and original thinker with many unorthodox theories. He was often ridiculed for his evolutionist view that men were descended from apes, and had worn away their tails by their habit of sitting on them. He wrote a long, diffuse, but most interesting book called *The Origin and Progress of Language*.[2] He said in it many things that would meet with approval today, for instance that language cannot be studied apart from the society in which it is spoken, and that speech had its origin in the cries of command or exhortation which were 'necessary in carrying on work by joint consent'.[3] But he also committed himself to the rash remark that English when spoken contains no variation, from syllable to syllable, of pitch. 'The music of our language', he wrote, 'is nothing better than the music of a drum, in which we perceive no difference except that of louder or softer.'[4]

Steele, at the request of his friend, Sir John Pringle, President of the Royal Society and once Professor of Moral Philosophy at Edinburgh, sent Monboddo an essay attacking this view; and Monboddo's reply, and Steele's further arguments, make up Steele's book as actually published. Monboddo finished by admitting he was wrong, and retracted gracefully with expressions of admiration for Steele's analysis and notation.

---

[1] James Burnet, Lord Monboddo, was born in Kincardineshire in 1714 and died in Edinburgh in 1799. There was a famous encounter between him and Dr Johnson in 1773, during Johnson and Boswell's highland tour, at Monboddo's Kincardineshire house. The two famous scholars did not admire each other.

[2] Published in Edinburgh in six volumes between 1773 and 1792.

[3] Cf. the similar views put forward by G. A. de Laguna, *Speech, Its Function and Development*, New Haven, 1927. Monboddo also held that 'language spoken may be said to be *living language*, compared with written language, which may be called *the dead letter*, being altogether *inanimate*, and nothing more than marks or signs of language' (Vol. IV, p. 170); he arrived, apparently independently of Sir William Jones, at the opinion that Greek, Latin and Sanscrit (which he learnt), as well as Teutonic, Persian and Celtic, are 'dialects of the same parent language'; and he distinguished between 'inclusive' and 'exclusive' personal pronouns. Many other opinions he held are strikingly contemporary.

[4] op. cit., Vol. II, p. 300.

Other people before Steele, of course, had noticed and commented on intonation in languages. Steele was not the discoverer of melody in English; but no one before him had attempted to examine it in such detail.

As I said just now, intonation follows established patterns; but these are not universal patterns—they vary from language to language and from dialect to dialect. 'Take three common men', writes Steele, 'one a native of Aberdeenshire, another of Tipperary, and the third of Somersetshire; and let them converse together in the English language, in the presence of any gentleman of the courtly tone of the metropolis; his ears will soon inform him, that every one of them talks in a tune very different from his own, and from each other.' This speech melody or tune gives a very different effect from that of song, because (again I quote Steele) 'the melody of speech moves rapidly up or down by slides, wherein no graduated distinction of tones or semitones can be measured by the ear; nor does the voice (in our language) ever dwell distinctly, for any perceptible space of time, on any certain level or uniform tone, except the last tone on which the speaker ends or makes a pause'. That people do not notice this, or are not aware of the details of it, is, he says, because 'the extreme familiarity existing between a man and his native language, makes him lose all sense of its features'.

The controversy with Monboddo started over the melody of speech, but Steele found he could not discuss this without going into the *measure* of speech, its rhythm in other words, also. This is a complex subject, and still today a matter of dispute, though Steele's views are very far from being outmoded.

The measure of speech, in prose as well as poetry, is governed, he maintained, by a '*pulsation* of emphatic and remiss', which divides it into *cadences* or bars. He claims that in English the cadences are of equal length, that is to say that the pulsation is *periodic*, or tends to be; and although doubt about what we are going to say next, and other things, may throw the regularity out for a moment, it always reasserts itself.

Steele does not explain very clearly what he means by this pulsation of emphatic and remiss, or heavy and light, as he also called it. He was always finding, when trying to explain this point, that people took him to mean by it an alternation of *loudness* and *softness*. But that was not his meaning. True, he said, a heavy, or as we should say, a *stressed* syllable *is* often louder than others. But not necessarily. In fact the 'emphatic impulse' which, falling on a syllable, makes it stressed, could, and often does, fall during a pause, in other words could be quite silent: for the recognition that pauses, or periods of silence, during speech are an essential part of its rhythmic effect is vital for Steele's theory (and, incidentally, is another point to which he converted Monboddo[1]).

These periodical pulsations of speech, falling sometimes on certain syllables, sometimes on silence, may seem fanciful. But modern research on the subject gives support to Steele, the regular pulsation turning out to be a pulse-like movement of the speaker's lung-muscles controlling the output of air.[2] Support is also found for the view, implicit in Steele's theories, that rhythm is not something to be found in the *sounds* of speech, but rather in the muscular movements of the speaker, and the listener's sympathetic knowledge of those movements: Steele speaks of 'this instinctive communication of periodic impulse', meaning that it is not necessarily audible as such.

In the illustration at the top of page 40 Steele shows what he means. It is a piece of ordinary conversation in which he has marked the rhythm very exactly; and he claims two things, first that the way it is marked is a perfectly natural way to say it, and secondly that the emphatic impulses come at regular intervals.[3]

That the regularity does not produce monotony is due to the recurrence of pauses, and also to the next point Steele sought to establish: that great variety is given within the regularity by

---

[1] Monboddo wrote, in a letter to Steele (reproduced in *Prosodia Rationalis*, p. 177), 'I must own myself fully convinced, that the pauses make an essential part of the rhythm of speech.'

[2] See P. Ladefoged, 'Syllables and Stress', *Miscellanea Phonetica*, III, 1958, and also the two preceding papers in the present volume.

[3] This piece of conversation was read aloud, at this point in the broadcast, by Mr J. C. Catford.

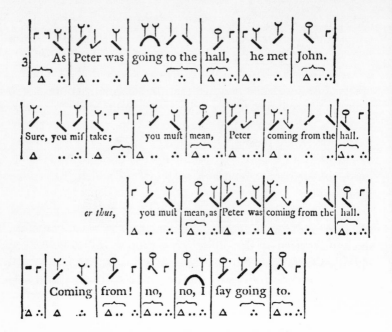

wide variation in the length of syllables. Here Steele's notation can show very small differences. For example, he gives Denham's well-known lines on the Thames as follows:

But he points out that Garrick preferred to say

—a subtle and individual difference of pause and syllable length which yet does not change the 'regular pulsation'.

I have not time to say much about the symbols themselves. They must have been a trial to the printer (it took him a week to set a single sheet), but they are not really as complex as they look. Very naturally, Steele had recourse to the only other notation where comparable things had been dealt with, that of music. In the complete form of his notation, which is used in the first passage above, he places above each syllable a symbol rather like a musical note, the top of which shows, by its shape, any one of seven degrees of length or quantity, and the bottom of which shows the slides of pitch variation. Musical rests indicate the pauses, and marks underneath the text, together with the bar lines, show the beats of emphatic and remiss. In some of his texts he used other marks to show variations in loudness. Thus five features of speech, missing from ordinary writing, could find expression in this notation. However, when he was discussing *measure* Steele often omitted the signs for *melody*.

Steele said that 'our natural elementary sounds, and the melody and measure of speech, are parts of the same subject'. That subject has for the last hundred years been called Phonetics; and in phonetic terminology the melody and measure are often called the *prosodic features* of speech, which means the features of the syllable. They are also the features which are important for *prosody* in the more usual sense of the word. Not many phoneticians have ventured into prosody (neither have many prosodists ventured into phonetics); but Steele, who may fairly enough be called a phonetician, held strong views on the subject, though they have never attracted much attention. English verse is often said to depend on *stress*. Steele's agreement with this was qualified by the special sense he attached to stress—the 'emphatic impulse'— which enabled him to regard a line of verse as perfectly regular when it was short of the number of stressed *syllables* which in theory it ought to contain, but had pauses for a compensating number of silent stresses to fall on (a thing which, he points out, happens commonly enough in music). Thus Steele objects to Monboddo's statement that the first line of *Paradise Lost* contains the five accented syllables *man's*, *dis*, *be*, *and*, *fruit*. 'To give it proper expression', Steele says, it should sound like this:[1]

Of | man's | first diso|bedience | ∧ and the | fruit

He also says that all verse supposed to contain five cadences or feet per line really 'required the time of six', thus anticipating the ideas of Coventry Patmore, who held that all verse had an *even* number of feet per line. We find, in fact, that Steele's transcription of the first three lines of *Paradise Lost* contains eighteen cadences or feet.

Steele had considerable discussion with David Garrick over his theories, and he indicates in his book how the great actor delivered the opening of the famous soliloquy from *Hamlet*. Steele does not, of course, give any indication of Garrick's accent, and we have no means of knowing it exactly. We do know that Garrick, like Dr Johnson, came from Lichfield, but it is not likely that he preserved, in the way that Johnson did, many of the distinguishing features of that locality. For one thing, Garrick used to amuse his friends by giving imitations of Johnson's accent, and he would not have done so, we may imagine, if he had still been vulnerable himself. Johnson said of his own accent, 'little aberrations are of no disadvantage', and in any case he claimed that the people of Lichfield spoke the purest English. He always said, for instance, *theer* for 'there', *heerd* for 'heard', and *woonse* for 'once'. Garrick himself, we are told by Fanny Burney, always said *shupreme* and *shuperior* for 'supreme' and 'superior', as did all Lichfield people— a pronunciation which had once been generally fashionable in the earlier eighteenth century, but was no longer normal in London. But we may suppose that for the most part 'little aberrations' of a markedly local character would hardly do for an actor in Garrick's position: he almost certainly had had to normalize his pronunciation to 'the courtly tone of the metropolis'.

The 'melody and measure', however, that is to say the length of syllables, the pauses, the stresses, the intonation and the variations in loudness, are indicated with great exactness; and

---

[1] Replacing Steele's notation by the simpler one explained in Ch. III.

they are very like what anybody might say today. This is, in a way, the most remarkable thing about the transcription. As Steele wrote, 'all nations are continually changing both their language and their pronunciation', and in matters of accent many languages—English especially—change fairly rapidly. But there are reasons for thinking that rhythm and intonation are very stable, in spite of the fact that an individual coming into a strange district will be likely to copy the local intonation quicker than he copies anything else. It seems that intonation, though very susceptible to outside influences, when left to itself persists almost unchanged; whereas the articulate sounds of speech will gradually alter whatever the circumstances.

Garrick spoke the whole soliloquy, according to Steele, 'with little or no distinction of piano and forte, but nearly uniform, and with something below the ordinary force'.

Lord Monboddo wrote in a letter to Steele, 'I am very glad to hear that your experiment upon Mr Garrick's declamation succeeded so well. Actors are the only artists that cannot eternize themselves by their works; but you have fallen upon a way to make Garrick live as long as his Shakespeare.'

The melody and measure of speech are very much a *personal*, as well as a social thing. There are established patterns, in rhythm and intonation, for each language or dialect, as much a *part* of that language as its articulate sounds or its grammar. But within these patterns, or 'norms', there is room for great individual variation, variation which expresses our personality and our feelings and emotions of the moment. Through these features spoken language is always *tied* closely to its immediate occasion, to the situation and to the persons participating.

The whole object of written language is to be *free* of any immediate context, whether personal or situational, and that is why it dispenses with systematic indication of intonation and rhythm, only giving the vaguest of hints in the form of question marks, commas, and so on. But this means that the written languages of the past can never reveal to us living speech, the speech of individuals, however skilful philologists may be at reconstructing the articulate sounds (and, with the help of phoneticians, they are very skilful). What a language really *sounds* like is this missing part—missing for ever before the invention of the gramophone, except for the fortunate and almost unique indications left us by Joshua Steele.

6

Forgotten phoneticians

Early writers on phonetics and alphabetics have usually had attention paid to them only in so far as they throw light on the pronunciation of their time. Writers who offer little evidence for this purpose, whatever their interest as linguistic thinkers, have received correspondingly little attention. There is, in fact, a firm opinion in some quarters that before about 1830 there was no such thing as phonetics. There was no such word, it is true; but something very like the thing has existed for a long time.

To underrate early writers on phonetics is probably really a nineteenth-century trait, dating from the time when they were all lumped together as 'orthoepists'; and nowadays many are being rehabilitated or rediscovered. Some while ago, for example, H. G. Fiedler drew attention[1] to Robert Robinson, a most remarkable early phonetician, whose previous neglect, included as he is in Watt's *Bibliotheca Britannica* (1824) under 'Pronunciation', is quite inexplicable. Since the appearance of Fiedler's article, very interesting manuscripts of Robinson's have been discovered, and the Society's *Transactions* for 1947 contain a valuable study of these by E. J. Dobson. And fairly recently Professor H. Kökeritz has exhibited the merits of William Tiffin and Mather Flint.[2]

---

[1] In Bulletin No. 15 of the Modern Humanities Research Association, November 1936.

[2] 'English Pronunciation as described in Shorthand Systems of the 17th and 18th Centuries', *Studia Neophilologica*, vol. vii, Uppsala, 1935; *Mather Flint on Early Eighteenth-Century Pronunciation*, Uppsala, 1944.

Paper read to the Philological Society on 5 June 1948, at Cambridge, and published in the Society's *Transactions* for 1948. A few extra footnotes have been added.

Professor J. R. Firth, in a paper to the Society in 1945,[1] made clear the greatness of past English achievement in the field of phonetics. The present paper is intended as a sort of supplement to his. Professor Firth dealt with the broad stream of the English tradition; most of my subjects, however, had little influence on either their contemporaries or their successors. They are admittedly, in fact, not of the first importance; but they all, I feel, have something of interest to offer, though they are not to be found in the usual bibliographies, histories of pronunciation, and other authorities where they have a right to expect to be. I have, perhaps, been rather tolerant in applying the term 'phonetician' to all of them, and if one or two were alive and publishing today I, for one, should resent their use of such a title. However, since I think they have all been forgotten beyond their deserts, the flattery may be indulged as some recompense for unjust neglect.

1

John Wilkins, at the beginning of that chapter of his *Essay towards a Real Character* (1668) which deals with 'the Philosophy of Articulate Sounds',[2] acknowledges the 'favour and good hap' he has had 'to peruse from their private papers, the distinct Theories of some other Learned and Ingenious persons, who have with great judgment applyed their thoughts to this enquiry'; and a note in the margin says these persons were Dr William Holder and Mr Lodowick. Wilkins adds that in each of their papers 'there are several suggestions that are new, out of the common rode, and very considerable'.

Professor Firth has done justice to that very remarkable and modern thinker William Holder. Francis Lodowick or Lodwick is to be the first subject of my paper today, and he is forgotten not only as a phonetician, but as a thinker on all problems of language. He lived at a time when almost everybody who was anybody had tried his hand at inventing a shorthand, a phonetic alphabet, and a universal language, and Lodwick was a pioneer in all these fields.

---

[1] 'The English School of Phonetics', *Transactions*, 1946.
[2] Part III, chapter X.

The Rev. Cave Beck, who published his *Universal Character* in 1657, usually gets the credit for being the earliest in England to bring out a universal language; but Lodwick had already published two books on the subject before Beck's book appeared. The first of these, *A Common Writing*, came out in 1647; it is occasionally mentioned, though few people seem to have read it (I have seen it described as a shorthand, and also as a work on phonetics, to neither of which it bears any resemblance). The second, little more than a pamphlet, seems to be quite unknown—perhaps owing to an eccentricity in the British Museum catalogue. Both these books by Lodwick[1] are of great interest, and not only on account of their early date; but I do not intend to discuss them on this occasion. It is worth mentioning in passing, however, that no less an authority than George Dalgarno thought well of Lodwick's work in this field. In a letter to Samuel Hartlib, dated

---

[1] The title-pages of the two books are as follows: (1) A Common Writing: Whereby two, although not understanding one the others Language, yet by the helpe thereof, may communicate their minds one to another. Composed by a Well-willer to Learning. Printed for the Author, 1647. (2) The Ground-Work, or Foundation Laid (or so intended), For the Framing of a New Perfect Language: And an Vniversall or Common Writing. And presented to the consideration of the Learned, By a Well-willer to Learning. Printed, Anno 1652.

Although these works have been attributed to Samuel Hartlib, there can be little doubt that Francis Lodwick is the author. The preface to the first is signed 'F.L.W.', and it excuses 'the harshnesse of the stile' on the grounds that 'this work commeth not from a Scholar, but a mechanick'. Francis Lodwick's notebooks, which are among the Sloane MSS. in the British Museum, contain much of the same material, especially the pages headed 'of an universall Reall Caracter' in Sloane 897.

The catalogue of the Shorthand Collection in the New York Public Library attributes *A Common Writing* to Lodwick, saying that the B.M. Catalogue, 'while using secondary entries under Hartlib and the initials of the preface, places the main entry under Lodowyck'. This, however, is not so; and *The Ground-Work* receives no mention under Lodowyck, though it appears as a secondary entry under F.L.W. (the main entry being under the title). Halkett and Laing (1926-34) accept the attribution to Lodwick of *A Common Writing*, but do not mention *The Ground-Work*.

Of the various spellings used by his contemporaries, 'Lodwick' seems to have been the commonest, and I have used it in this paper.

20 April 1657,[1] Dalgarno relates how he was shown Cave Beck's *Universal Character* in manuscript, before publication, by John Wilkins, who had been given it for criticism; Dalgarno found it, he said, 'nothing else, but an Enigmaticall waye of writing ye English Language', not an unjust description. He goes on to write to Hartlib, 'I have another Treatise by me, wch was put forth ye yeare of God 1647. to that same purpose, wch doth farre exceed ye other', and there can be no doubt that this refers to Lodwick's *Common Writing*. It is true that he adds that it 'comes very farre short of doeing ye thing', but in his advance publicity for his own *Ars Signorum* (1661) Dalgarno always mentions Lodwick, together with Bacon, Comenius, Seth Ward, William Petty, and others, as an authority on the subject of universal language.[2] Lodwick was one of those whose contributions ('no one less than £1, no one more than £10') enabled Dalgarno to complete his researches;[3] and he was also a member of the small committee charged by the Royal Society to continue Wilkins's work on a real character, after the latter's death, the others being the great scientists John Ray and Robert Hooke, together with Andrew Paschall and Thomas Pigott.[4]

It is difficult to get information about Lodwick's life. He seems to have been so well known to his contemporaries that nobody, not even John Aubrey, thought it worth while to record any particulars of him. The *D.N.B.* ignores him. Apart from the facts that he was a merchant of Dutch origin who lived in London, was elected a Fellow of the Royal Society in November 1681 and sworn of the Council in December 1686, lived a long life and knew a great number of people, I have been able to find out practically nothing about him. The catalogue of his private library is in the British Museum,[5] and it is an impressive collection

---

[1] A copy of this letter is in the British Museum, MS. Sloane 4377, f. 148.

[2] MS. Sloane 4377 contains several printed circulars issued by Dalgarno.

[3] See the note at the beginning of *Ars Signorum*.

[4] John Aubrey, *Brief Lives*, ed. Andrew Clark, 1898, vol. ii, p. 302.

Andrew Paschall and John Aubrey are said to have worked out a phonetic alphabet together; see 'Scholarship and Small-Talk', by Oliver Lawson Dick, *The Listener*, 20 November 1947, p. 904.

[5] MSS. Sloane 855 and 859.

of works on language, and covers as well a wide range of other subjects. He was clearly an interesting and versatile man, and I am hoping to produce a more detailed study of him. For the present I must confine myself to his ideas on phonetics.

I do not know what the 'private papers' which Lodwick lent to Wilkins were; they may have been destroyed in the Great Fire, with William Holder's notes, and the rest of the contents of Wilkins's study.[1] The evidence that survives of his phonetic speculations consists mainly of his shorthand, and his notes on phonetic transcription.

His shorthand, which apparently dates from about 1650, was worked out in both English and Dutch versions (the latter being, I believe, the first Dutch shorthand invented). It was never ·published, but it is preserved in two notebooks in the British Museum, MSS. Sloane 897 and 932. It is based on pairing voiced and voiceless consonants, one character being given to each pair. All the consonants of Dutch and English, except [ŋ], are included. The vowels are shown by disjoined dots, rather as in Pitman; or by writing a following consonant in varying positions in relation to a preceding consonant. The whole system is on a strictly phonetic basis. I have not found any connected texts written in it, and possibly it was not very fast, though it was short enough. However, it deserves to rank with Tiffin, Lyle, and Holdsworth and Aldridge as a pre-Pitman attempt to base short-hand purely on the spoken language.

Lodwick's phonetic notation tells us much more about his ideas on phonetics. It was published in the *Philosophical Transactions* of the Royal Society in 1686, with the title 'An Essay Towards an Universal Alphabet'. But it was worked out, and was circulating in manuscript, many years before that: Robert Hooke records in his diary in November 1673 that he had been lent Lodwick's new universal alphabet.[2] There are two manuscript versions in the British Museum in Sloane 897 and 932; in one of these,

---

[1] See *Supplement to the Philosophical Transactions of July 1670*, London, 1678.
[2] *The Diary of Robert Hooke 1672-1680*, ed. H. W. Robinson and W. Adams, London, 1935, p. 69.

anticipating a modern fashion in word-formation, he refers to his 'universalphabeth'.

His aim, he says in the published article, is to provide an alphabet 'which should contain an Enumeration of all such Single Sounds or Letters as are used in any Language'. 'All single sounds ought to have single and distinct characters', and no one character shall 'have more than one Sound, nor any one Sound be expressed by more than one Character'.

Unlike many others who have attempted the same thing, Lodwick was modest in his claims. 'Altho', he wrote, 'this my attempt be not new, yet I hope what herein I have done will not be unuseful.' By means of an alphabet such as his, he considered, the pronunciation of any language can be described, and the true sounds of any language may be perpetuated. Moreover, children brought up on it will be able without difficulty to pronounce any language they may need to learn.

There are two very interesting features of the notation. The first is that it does not have the letters of the roman alphabet as a basis, 'because people so long accustomed or habituated to the corrupt and differing expressions of the present characters, will be always subject on the sight of the old, to give them those sounds they have been used to, and to spell words according to their old and corrupt custom, whatsoever rules shall be set to the contrary. I have therefore in the following Table given a new set of literal characters, both consonantal and vocal.'

This new set of characters was so designed that it provided similarities in articulation with analogous modifications of the symbols, 'the more regularly to sort them into classes, and to express the derivation of Letters of the same organe, the one from the other'. Many other people have had the same idea. Melville Bell worked it out very fully in his Visible Speech. A century before Lodwick, Honorat Rambaud of Marseilles had invented an elaborate notation on comparable principles.[1] Robert Robinson's alphabet (1617) was also on a non-roman basis, but the few analogies he provides between articulation

---

[1] *La Declaration des Abus que lon commet en escriuant*, Lyons, 1578.

The Universall Alphabet. 137

The Table of Confonants

The Table of Vowels

The Lords Prayer in Englifh.

PLATE I.—From Francis Lodwick's 'Essay towards an Universal Alphabet', *Philosophical Transactions*, Number 182, Vol. 16, p. 137, 26 June 1686.

and shape of character are unsystematic. Apart from one of the notations of John Wilkins, which is mentioned below, this experiment of Lodwick's seems to be the earliest of its kind in England. It suffers from the same defect as all its 'representational' predecessors and successors: the letters are far too like one another, and reading becomes a painful and laborious process.

The second interesting feature is that the transcription is, in effect, *syllabic*, the vowel symbols being diacritics written over the preceding consonant. This is important in Lodwick's theories, and is based on what many of us would consider sound (and modern) principles of teaching children to read. 'The usual method of teaching to spell is to dismember every syllable (of more than one letter) into many syllables, by expressing every letter apart, and syllabically.' 'How preposterous this method is', he comments; children should be taught 'to express every syllable entire at first sight', and his notation will tend to prevent syllables being 'dismembered'.

One of the three types of phonetic notation described by John Wilkins is designed to show related sounds by analogies in shape of character.[1] It is also a syllabic notation, and it seems possible that this is one of the places where Wilkins was influenced bv Lodwick's 'private papers'.

It should be noted that Lodwick's alphabet is a *universal* one, intended to be capable of transcribing all languages. Plate I shows it as it appeared in the *Philosophical Transactions*. The consonants are arranged in horizontal 'ranks' and vertical 'files', that is to say they are classified by place and manner. The first rank is occupied by what he calls the 'primitives'; the others being 'derivatives' which 'have the same posture of the mouth, but with som differences'. The 'primitives' are the voiced plosives, the other ranks being voiceless plosive, nasal, voiced fricative, and voiceless fricative, in that order. Semi-vowels and liquids do not fit comfortably into this scheme, and they are given a file each to themselves (numbers 7 to 11). Of these, only [l] is provided with a voiceless equivalent. Lodwick gives no explanation of the con-

---

[1] See p. 376 of his *Essay towards a Real Character*.

sonant in file 12, or of the solitary occupant of rank 6, in file 2, but the former, it is reasonable to suppose from its Hebrew equivalent and the way it is used in the text, represents a glottal stop; the latter, as is clear from Lodwick's notebooks, was to be used in transcribing nasalized vowels.

The files from 1 to 6 are, respectively, bilabials, dentals, palatals, velars, labiodentals, and alveolars. Where possible Lodwick has given an equivalent in roman letters of the sounds, but has not tried to find equivalents for bilabial fricatives, alveolar plosives, or labiodental plosives. He comments on these sounds that they are 'so like in pronunciation to some others in the Table, that the difference would be too nice for common discernment'.

The values of most of the vowel diacritics can be discovered with the help of the text; they do not seem to be arranged with any method. In his earlier drafts Lodwick had tried several different arrangements, some of which appear better than the published one. Incidentally, the earlier drafts had more consonants provided for—a 'more guttural expression' of the velar file, for example, by which uvular sounds must be intended.

Stress is marked by a short horizontal line under the stressed syllable. The normal punctuation marks are to be used, with the addition of ¿ to indicate irony, and ¡ for emphasis.

The essay was thought important enough to be reproduced almost in full in the abridgement of the *Philosophical Transactions*.[1] The Royal Society, however, did Lodwick small honour, sixty years later, by having his alphabet reported on by John Byrom, F.R.S., the shorthand inventor. Byrom knew little of phonetics, and failed to understand Lodwick's classification of sounds or the purpose of his notation. He consequently reported adversely, and put forward an alternative, and very poor, classification of sounds of his own.[2]

Since then nothing has been heard of Lodwick; but I think he probably had considerable influence on his contemporaries.

---

[1] *The Philosophical Transactions and Collections to the End of the Year 1700 Abridg'd and Dispos'd under General Heads*, by John Lowthorp, London, 1705, vol. iii, pp. 373-9.

[2] *Philosophical Transactions*, vol. 45, p. 401, June 1748.

Robert Hooke was one of Lodwick's best friends, and the records in Hooke's diaries[1] of innumerable coffee-house conversations show how often Lodwick talked with such famous figures as Halley, Aubrey, Robert Boyle, Christopher Wren, and others less well remembered, about shorthand, 'Chinese language tones',[2] universal character, the orthography of music, and all the other linguistic topics of interest in those days.

2

My next two subjects are the authors of two very early eighteenth-century pamphlets; they are less interesting, and a great deal more forgotten. The first wrote a pamphlet with the odd title *Magazine*, published in 1703, and printed in London for the author, price sixpence. The author gives his initials as G. W. on the title page; I have been unable to identify him with any writer of the time. The pamphlet is octavo, of 32 pages, and I know of only one copy, which is in the Pitman Library.[3]

The full title reads: 'Magazine, or, Animadversions on the English Spelling; observing the Contradictions of the English Letters Warring themselves against themselves, and one with another, by Intrusions and Usurpations; with Amendment offer'd. For the Benefit of all Teachers and Learners, Writers and Readers, Composers and Scriveners, whether Strangers or Natives, who are concern'd with our English Tongue.' G. W. is, in fact, a spelling reformer. Except for a brief comment by myself in *Le Maître Phonétique*,[4] he has never been noticed before; no bibliography mentions him. Any early spelling reformer has something to contribute to our knowledge of the history of English pronunciation, and perhaps to our knowledge of early ideas on phonetics

[1] *The Diary of Robert Hooke 1672-1680*, ed. H. W. Robinson and W. Adams, London, 1935; the diary from 1688 to 1693 is included in vol. x of R. T. Gunther's *Early Science in Oxford*, Oxford, 1935.

[2] Hooke uses this expression in the entry for 14 May 1679. The earliest use of *tone* in this sense given by the *O.E.D.* in 1763.

[3] It is now available as Publication Number 70 of *The Augustan Reprint Society*, Los Angeles, 1958.

[4] No. 59, July-September 1937, p. 34.

and alphabetics. G. W. has not, perhaps, very much to contribute; but so far he has not had any chance to offer it.

He writes in a racy but clumsy style, full of jokes and obscure allusions, and the very careless printing does not make it any easier to understand. Only random indications of his ideas for amendment are given, the pamphlet being mostly devoted to showing how badly traditional English spelling is in need of it. His criticisms are the usual ones, though not always expressed in the usual manner: 'B is overplus in Lamb, thumb, debt, doubt; and what need is there of these unnecessary bees; scarce one in a Parish besides the Parson thinks the two last come of Latin words, debitum and dubito.' 'Why is not i and e cast out of praise and raise, and e from wife and strife, which adorn the words no more than Beauty-spots do a Whore's Face.' 'If ae, eo, ie, and ea be diphthongs, and lawfully marry'd by Banes, or Licens, I'm sure it is but an half char-marriage, for they (for a just impediment) never bed together.' 'Our Children are not Witches, that they should guess to Read right by the Letter, such stuff as this.' 'Which thing hath made a many Foreigners (and no marvel at all) of all the Neighbouring Nations to throw away their Books and Study in English.'

There is no systematic statement of the reforms he thinks necessary, his scheme in detail being promised for a later work which may or may not have appeared, but of which no trace can now be found. In brief, his remedy is: 'more Letters would do well in the Alfabet, but fewer in most words'; but although his reform would be radical, he points out that 'when we speak of altering the Letters, we alter not, but establish and settle the known speech, which is no more but to alter or remove the sign when it directeth to the wrong house, but the Inn all the while is the same'. In the provision of new letters, and in determining the values of the old ones, he starts from a curious principle. Most reformers have thought it necessary to establish a close relationship between the *sound* and the *name* of a letter, and they have done this by basing the name on the sound, as in the Phonic method of teaching reading. G. W. went the other way about it. 'If you had said HURH spells Church, and GUG spells Judge', he remarks, 'I could easily believe it'; and what he in fact does, is to base the sounds of the letters *h* and *g* on their traditional names, making them [tʃ] and [dʒ]. He then, of course, has to invent new letters for the sounds [h] and [g], and he obtains them by reversing *h* and inverting *g*.

Five other new letters are provided, all obtained by inversion: ɹ for [θ], ɔ for [ð], ʌ for [ŋ], ʃ for [ʃ], and ʍ with its modern I.P.A. value. J is used for [ʒ], c for [k], and x for [ks]. All his symbols are provided with capitals, D being the capital of ɔ, and ◻ of d.

Most of these new letters, however, are apparently makeshifts, the new types required being too much for the printer—one of them is described as 'the sign Taurus with a foot-ball between his horns'. G. W. also suggests, but makes no use of in the pamphlet, 'a low apostrophe, as high as the bodies of the letters' for the vowel in *bit*. Long vowels are to be shown by placing what he calls a 'cambril', or circumflex, over them.

His new letters, and old ones with his new values, are used sporadically throughout the pamphlet, apparently whenever he remembered and the printer noticed. There are, however, a few texts entirely transcribed in his reformed spelling, the longest being thirty-two lines of doggerel.[1] From these, and from various incidental remarks, some interesting points of pronunciation emerge. He uses the digraph au in the following words: hau (*how*), taunz (*towns*), auns (*ounce*), paundz (*pounds*), nau (*now*), aur (*our*); but there is no corresponding digraph ai. uu is used in fuul (*fool*), buux (*books*), tuu (*too*), cruuced (*crooked*); and he has a remarkable statement to the effect that the letter *o* in normal spelling is 'often us'd for a triphthong ouu', as in *bone, stone, doore, through, wo, whore, sore, more. f*, he says, is unpronounced in *mastiff*, and *t* is spoken instead of *f* in *handful, armful, sackful*.[2] [ʒ] is given in *measure, osier, hosier, easier, azure*. 'The Countryman of the North in Apron and Iron, pronounce o after r, and we before it.'

In a very useful survey[3] of the evidence concerning the develop-

---

[1] Twelve of these lines were reproduced in the *Maître Phonétique*, loc. cit.

[2] cf. Wright's *English Dialect Dictionary*, s.v. 'hantle'.

[3] In his *Mather Flint*, pp. 136-52.

ment of *kn-* and *gn-*, Dr Helge Kökeritz observes that 'only foreign grammarians report the intermediate stages *tn* and *dn*'. G. W., however, has the transcriptions tnav[1] (*knave*), tno (*know*), tnu (*knew*). He gives *cloaks*, moreover, as tlox (Robert Robinson also regularly has initial *tl* and *dl*).

G. W. has many observations of interest, in addition to his animadversions on spelling. He is tolerant of dialects: 'If one be in the North or West, he had best speak as they do, that he may be readily understood, which is the end of speech.' And again, 'many delight to hear different dialects (as the Grecians did) so they did but understand one another, though some precise Females do condemn all but their own finical pronunciation'. The reputation of Englishmen as linguists was better then than it is now: ''Tis thought by some of the Learned, that English is the hardest Language in the World; for that Foreigners coming over, being past Children, never have our speech right, but may be discern'd to be no English born, whereas we after a short abode in out-Lands, speak their Tongue as well as Natives'.

He disapproves of spelling pronunciations, which he calls 'a false finical speech according to the Letters, being illeterately litterate'.

It is still true today that 'there was as good reason for amendment an Hundred Years ago, as there is now, and will be as good reason an Hundred years hence to delay the amendment, as their is now'.

It is a pity that we are not in possession of the sequel to *Magazine*, the 'ensuing Batl-dur'[2] as he calls it. G. W. seems to have been singularly little under the influence of the traditional spelling and, in spite of his style and his inefficient printer, it might have had much to teach us.

3

The second early eighteenth-century pamphlet is anonymous, and lacks even the author's initials. Its title is 'The Needful Attempt, to make Language and Divinity Plain and Easie', and it was

---

[1] Misprinted tnaʌ.

[2] i.e. battledore, or horn-book.

printed in London by John Morphew and published in 1711.
It is twenty-one pages long, and concludes with the phrase
'Dhe End auf dhe Furst Part'. I do not know whether there ever
was a second part; the first is concerned with the making easy
of language only. The pamphlet has been referred to before by
Isaac Pitman in his periodical *The Speler*, in 1895, and by myself
in the *Maître Phonétique*, in the article which discussed G. W.'s
Magazine; otherwise it has apparently escaped notice.

The author is another spelling reformer, more intelligible but
less amusing than G. W. Remarkably enough, he too is aware
of spelling pronunciations—'speaking too much according to the
present way of spelling, which is very foppish and ridiculous'.
He brings forward the usual arguments against the traditional
spelling and in favour of reform, and then expounds his own
remedies. He introduces no new letters. Among the consonants,
he discards *c* altogether; *g* is used for [g], and *j* for [dʒ]. *qu* is
retained in its traditional value, and so is *x*. Additional symbols
are provided by means of digraphs: *th*, *dh*, *sh*, *ng*, *wh*. [tʃ] is
usually written *tsh*, though the puzzling digraph *kh* is used
initially. In transcribing vowels, he employs an acute (sometimes
a circumflex) accent to denote length, and introduces the digraphs
ai, *au*, *ee*, *oi*, *oo*, *ou*, and the trigraph *eea*. He considers capital
letters unnecessary, though he continues to use them.

The result is a very practical and simple phonetic spelling,
and fourteen of the twenty-one pages of the pamphlet are printed
in it—quite a considerable connected text. It is not one of those
systems which aim at merely reducing the anomalies of traditional
spelling as far as possible—an *amended spelling*, to use Zachrisson's
term. The *Needful Attempt* completely respells every word in
accordance with strict conventions carried out with admirable
consistency. The following are specimens:

(p. 8) Grammar beeing to teeatsh, az speedili az kan bee, dhe
art of speling, spéking, ríting, and reeding a Languaj rítli; and
if it bee a spóken Languaj, akaurding to dhe móst usual wai of
spéking it; mi Bísnez dherfor I kount iz, to teatsh, az breefli and
plainli az I kan, whaut iz nesesari to dhe rít speling, and spéking,

and ríting, and reeding Inglish az tiz spók. And dhat, I think, iz, furst, to teatsh dhe Leters (bóth *Vouels* and *Kaunsonants*) and dhe rít pronounsing auf dhem. 2. Aul dhe *Silabuls*; aul dhat can be mád, bóth bi plásing dhe *Kaunsonants* befór, and after dhe *Vouels*. 3. Som fú nesesari Things about Words and Sentenses.

No mór, I think, iz needful in an *Inglish Grammar*; but beecaus som Lairners must (faur som tím, if naut aulwais) bee veri redi and perfekt in reeding and pronounsing rítli, aul Words auf dhe present wai auf speling; dherfor wee shud indeed hav, if it quud[1] bee, anodher Grammar, to teatsh hou to spék and pronouns aul Words auf dhe present wai auf speling (az faur ríting and speling um so, dher mai bee nó nesesiti, dhat I kno auf at present, faur ani to lairn dhat) but our present wai auf speling iz so veri unrezonabul and irregular, dhat tiz impausibul, I beeleev, to compóz a Grammar neer sufishent to teeatsh a Lairner dhe present wai auf pronounsing aul Words so speld.

(p. 12) But bi khanjing our present wai auf spéling to our present wai auf spéking; and bí dhe fú odher Alteráshons heer menshond, 'twil bee an eeasi and shaurt Work, I think, to kompós an exakt Gramar to our Languaj, wheerbi, with a litul teeatshing, to lairn it very easili and veri soon.

And faur dhe jeneraliti auf Peepul (hoo hav naut tím naur need to reed mutssh) a veri fú gwud[2] Books, in dhis nu wai of speling mai be sufishent, which I shal endevor dhai shal naut want.

And I beeleev móróver, dhat hoosoever, shal lairn, in dhe furst plás, dhis wai dhat I now propôs, mai afterwards, if dhai wil, bi dheir ón Praktis and Aubserváshon, with very litul aur nó teeatshing, beecóm ábul, mutssh sooner dhan Peepul hidherto hav bin, to reed wel ani odher Book aulso auf dhe present speling.

(p. 15) To proseed nou about dhe *Kaunsonants* auf dhis Gramar;

---

[1] cf. the author's statement elsewhere in the pamphlet that *w* occurs before the *u* in *bull, pull, bush, push.*

[2] See above.

whitsh ar dhe sám az hidherto, onli wanting dhe *c*; and dho I plás um heer, furst, in dhair yúsual aurder, faur dhe sák auf sutsh az mai hav beegun to lairn um so, and dherupaun mai find it difikult to lairn um oderwez; yet faur dhe beter and sooner lairning to rít um (whitsh I wud hav aul doo dhat kan, at furst lairning um) í think it best to plás um ódherwez too; furst the nín shaurt wonz, wheerauf dhe fív faurmer wil be eeasli mád be furst máking dhe *r*, on whitsh dhe rest depend; dhen dhe fív long dounwards, and dhen dhe six long upwards; auf aul whitsh dhe eeasist to be mád is plást furst, on whitsh aulso dhe rest depend, and are to be mád mutsh in lík maner.

Heer faulo dhe won and twenti kaunsonants, in dhair óld aurder; *b c d f g h j k l m n p q r s t v w x y z.*

Dhe twenti, in dhair nú aurder: *r n m v w t s x z j y ƿ q g l b h k f d.*

If dheez bee taut at furst bi dhe Náms auf *ra na ma va wa ta sa xa za ja ya ƿa qua ga la ba ha ka fa da*, dhai wud so, perhaps, bee mór eeasli lairnt, and dhe Speling mutsh mór eeasli. Faur, dhe very Náms auf dhe Leters wil teatsh whaut étsh Leter spels joind with *a* after it; az *ra-a ra*; *na-a na*, &c. and dhen twil eeasli be lairnt dhat *na-é* spels *né, na-í ní*, &c. So dhat neer háf dhe bisnes auf lairning to spel will be dun bi lairning dhe Leters bi dheez Náms.

I have made no emendations in the above extracts; many printer's errors are obvious.

Both *Magazine* and *The Needful Attempt* possibly contain useful indications of contemporary pronunciation, and they might be worth detailed examination by those whose business is with such things. Their authors are the only spelling reformers I have come across in the first half of the eighteenth century. The apparently unique copies are in the spelling reform and shorthand library formed by Sir Isaac Pitman, and I am greatly indebted to Mr I. J. Pitman, M.P.,[1] for the facilities I have been given in working with them, and for kindly providing me with photostats.

---

[1] Now Sir James Pitman.

4

A very reasonable theory has been put forward that phonetics started in England owing to the striking discrepancies between the way English is spelt and the way it is spoken: a new, speculative, approach to problems of pronunciation was forced on us because of the inadequacy of the traditional approach, derived from the classical grammarians, in the face of these discrepancies. The new approach was not, of course, recognized as a separate 'subject' until it received a new name and was thus distinguished from the branch of traditional grammar called orthography or orthoepy.

This theory was most remarkably anticipated by an eighteenth-century philosopher who published in 1773, under the name of Edward Search, a book called *Vocal Sounds*. In England, he said, we take language in more strongly by the eye than the ear. The consequent uncertainty concerning its sound 'has given birth to a new science added to the two well known before, orthography and philology, and which may be named philophony: the child lies as yet scarce half formed in the nursery of grammarians, but the tender nurture of it seems a fit employment for the Searches, for our family has been remarkable for the watchful ear, as well as the prying eye, ever since our great uncle Socrates heard the whispers of the dæmon sent from Jove'.

His suggested name, philophony, was not the one eventually adopted, but his fitness for the tender nurture of the subject is well borne out by the book, which is, moreover, one of the very few intentionally humorous works on general phonetics ever written.

The author's real name was Abraham Tucker. He was born in 1705, and was a country gentleman who lived in Betchworth Castle, near Dorking. He published books on philosophy under the names of Edward Search and Cuthbert Comment; they were very badly received during his lifetime, though it was not known until after his death that he was the author of them. *Vocal Sounds* was printed for private circulation in the year before his death, and two years after the author had become totally blind; he was able to continue to write legibly by means of a little machine he invented to guide his hand.

His character is well described by John Fyvie in *Noble Dames and Notable Men of the Georgian Era* (London, 1910): 'A man of an exceptionally happy temperament, amiable and benevolent in conduct, serene and cheerful in temper, no less distinguished from the squirearchy of his day by an unconquerable aversion both to fox-hunting and to place-hunting, and by a devotion to plain living and high thinking, than he is from most of the philosophers of that or any other day by the possession of a rich vein of quaint and quiet humour, which runs through and colours all his speculations, on even the highest and most sacred themes.'

Tucker's chief philosophical work, *The Light of Nature Pursued*, is very long (the first volumes came out in 1768; the concluding three volumes were brought out posthumously by his daughter), and this doubtless partly explains why it is little known. Nevertheless, as Fyvie says, 'it is difficult to understand how so rich a mine of suggestive thought and brilliant illustration can have been allowed to lie so long in obscurity'.[1] Among Tucker's many notable anticipations of modern thought were his belief that all our diseases may proceed from 'an imperceptible vermin swarming within us'; and his advocacy of the scientific study of the child-mind. It is really most extraordinary that Fyvie, in his account of Tucker's versatility and originality, makes no mention of the fact that he wrote a book on phonetics. *Vocal Sounds* is as original, as clearly thought out, and as amusing, as the rest of his work.

'I should have entitled my performance letters', Tucker wrote, 'but that I should then have been understood of letters written, or characters used upon paper; whereas my intention is to point out the letters spoken, or single sounds composing our syllables and words when we discourse with one another. But these two kinds of letters, the written and the spoken, do not always answer each other.' He is not, however, a spelling reformer, but points out correctly the need for a phonetic notation: 'It seems necessary to rectify our alphabet, not that I mean to alter the common manner of writing, but only to gratify the curiosity of such as may be desirous of analysing our language into its constituent elements.

---

[1] For another warm appreciation of Tucker's work, see pp. 260-3 of G. Saintsbury's *The Peace of the Augustans*, London, 1916.

and to furnish them with a set of characters whereby they might
express and distinguish every articulate sound that is current
among us.' He expresses a hope that the reader will not be
'frighted at reading such uncouth characters as I present him with'.
However, his notation, designed for English, contains only six
new letters, four for the consonants [θ, ð, ʃ, ŋ], and two for the
vowels [ə] or [ʌ], and [ɔ]. He uses *j* without a dot for [ʒ], and
c for [k]. The five vowel letters of the traditional alphabet are
given their 'Italian' values, and length is indicated by a dot over
the letter; the vowel in *bit* therefore is written *i* without a dot.
He suggests, but has no occasion to use, ʌ for the French vowel
[y]. 'I flatter myself', he says, 'that any person who would take
the pains to be acquainted with my alphabet, would be enabled
thereby to read any speech or composition in the same manner,
that is, the same articulate, I do not say the same tonical, musical,
or rather anti-musical sounds, as the speaker had delivered, or
the author would read it himself, and even to follow them through
whatever peculiarities of utterance they may have adopted.'
He does not provide very much in the way of connected transcriptions, but three pages of the book are devoted to a poem of his
own composition, each line being followed by a phonetic rendering.
Plate II illustrates one of these pages. Tucker records that while
at work upon it he found, as many others have experienced
when they first try phonetic transcription, that 'it required constant
close attention and subjected him to a continual hazard of
blunders'. A certain number of blunders, either his or the printer's,[1]
are still there, but it must be remembered that proof correction
must have presented a considerable problem to a blind author.

All his new symbols may be found in Plate II except the one
for [ŋ], which was not unlike the present I.P.A. symbol, being
the tail of a g added to an n. The printer was unable to put a
dot for length over the symbol for [ɔ], and has used àu for it
instead. The transcriptions 'cʋind' *kind*, 'bʋi' *by* will be noted;

---

[1] *Vocal Sounds* was printed by T. Jones, in Fetter Lane; the title-page adds
'and sold by T. Payne, at the Mews-gate', but there are reasons for thinking
it was never put on sale.

[48]

The language drawn from every day's dif-
    courfe,

" ẟi languedȝ dráun fræm everı déz difcórs,"

But cull'd with judgement. from that turbid
    fource :

" But culd uıẟ djudȝment fræm ẟat turbıdfurs :"

No low-bred phrafe, nor incoherence rude,

" No ló-bred fréz næwr incohirens rúd,"

Nor ungrammatic ftructure may intrude :

" Næwr ungramatic ftructıur mé intrúd :"

Nor affectation fpread her tawdry paint,

" Næwr afectéfıun fpred hur táudrı pént,"

Nor pedantry with mufty dulnefs taint :

" Næwr pedantrı uıẟ muftı dulnes tént :"

Yet knowledge or of fcience, or of men,

" ıet noledȝ æwr æwv fuiens, æwr æwv men,"

Itfelf unfeen, may prompt the tutor'd pen.

" ıtfelf unfin mé præmpt ẟı tutæwrd pen."

If argument be needful, let it prefs

" ıf arguıment be nidful let ıt pres"

With inborn weight, not urg'd with eagernefs :

" uıẟ ınbæwrn uét, næwt urdȝd uıẟ igurnes :"

If kind profeffions, fetch them from the heart,

" ıf cuınd profefıunz, fetfı ẟem fræm ẟı hárt,"

Nature's pure growth, unfabricate by art.

" Næuurz pıúr groþ, unfabrıccte buı árt."

PLATE II.—From *Vocal Sounds*, by Abraham Tucker (Edward Search),
London, 1773.

the diphthong was so represented by, among others, John Wilkins and Benjamin Franklin. Tucker gives elsewhere 'dȧı' as being the Suffolk pronunciation of *day*. u and ı are used for [w] and [j].

Tucker realizes that it is not easy to find out how sounds are made. 'One would think there could be nothing curious in telling people what they do every day, and every hour of the day; but experience testifies that we do not always advert upon things we perform by constant habit and in a manner mechanically; I have found difficulty in examining my own motions exactly, and have met with people who would hold an argument in what manner we both performed the same operation.' 'I find nothing is to be done by occasional observations, nor without preparing oneself by a thorough consideration, and making it the principal business of one's thoughts for some time.' His observation was very careful and painstaking (although he points out that 'it were endless, and indeed impossible, to describe the exact posture of our organs in making the vocal sounds'). He describes t as being made with 'the whole rim of the tongue against the gum, just behind the teeth'. He calls c, t, p, the 'silent stops, because their sound is instantaneous like the stroke of a hammer'. When they are final, 'at the end of a sentence perhaps when we have done speaking, the muscles of the tongue may relax a moment sooner than the breath ceases to push against the stop, whence issues forth a very faint blowing which might be called the ghost of an "h"'. 'The drawing the lips asunder, or hind part of the tongue from the roof of the mouth in order to pass from "p" or "c" to "t", may produce a little faintish smack.' The 'sonorous stops' g, d, b, are 'capable of being drawn out like the notes of an organ to a length proportionable to the cavity there is to receive the breath coming from the lungs', g being shortest and b longest. He describes the sounds [x, ɣ], which he says English must once have possessed, and the bilabial fricative [ɸ], which he thinks may have been the sound of Greek ϕ. 'There is scarce a language', he says, 'which has not some particular letter unknown to its neighbours.' Many 'tones and whines' exist also, for example in Chinese, 'so that it is impossible to frame a universal alphabet, unless one could know and find characters for all the various tones that are in currency among all nations upon earth'. Tucker's alphabet will confine itself 'to the articulation, not meddling with the various tones'.

There are noteworthy remarks concerning the pronunciation of his time. There can be little doubt that Tucker intends some sort of central vowel, [ə], by his symbol *v*. It is true that he uses it in both syllables of the word *cover*, but the identification of these two vowels may be found in other writers,[1] and is common enough in many types of English today. 'This short "*v*" ', says Tucker, 'is easiest pronounced of all the vowels . . . and therefore is a great favorite with my countrymen, who tho not lazy are very averse to trouble, wishing to do as much work with as little pains as possible.' 'We can draw it out to a great length upon particular occasions, as when the watchman calls "Past ten *v-v-v* clock", or when a man hesitates till he hits upon some hard name, as "This account was sent by Mr *v-v-v* Schlotzikoff, a Russian".' It may be heard in the words *there, beer, fire, more, poor, pure, our*, 'which we pronounce theʋr, bɪʋr, fʋɪʋr, moʋr, pʋʋr, pɪuʋr, ʋuʋr'; and in *sir, dirty*. Moreover, 'er is so like to "ʋr" that you cannot distinguish them unless when accented, for if one was to say "prospʋr, advʋrse, to join in friendly convʋrse" you would not perceive the changes, but "prospʋrity, advʋrsity, to convʋrse as friends", would offend your ear grievously'. 'There are none of the vowels but what are often changed into "ʋ" in common talk, tho preserving their genuine sound in a grave discourse, as in this sentence, " 'Tis frivolous to endeavour putting man or woman upon never stirring in London for fear of their cloaths being covered with soot", which at a teatable we should probably deliver thus, " 'Tis frivʋlʋs to endeavʋr putting man ʋr womʋn ʋpʋn nevʋr stʋrring in Lʋnʋn fʋr fear ʋf their cloaths being cʋvʋr'd with sʋt." '

The 'weak forms' for *or, upon, for, of*, in the preceding extract will be noticed; Tucker pointed out that 'the very small particles spoken hastily scarce ever retain their original sound, a farmer will tell you "ʋ hog wont stray so fʋr frʋm home ʋz ʋn ox ʋr ʋ flock *v* sheep".' Unfortunately, he does not use weak forms in the transcription of his poem, where he is very sparing of *v* altogether.

Concerning r he says: 'Upon rendering the end of the tongue limber, so that it will shake like a rag with the bellows, it will rattle out "r", but this requiring a strong stream of breath to perform, makes it the most laborious letter of all, and consequently as much out of our good graces as I said "*v*" was in them.' People drop the r, he says, in *furs, partial, servants, worst, worsted, backward*, and many other words; 'and whenever retained we speak it so gently that you scarce hear a single reverberation of the tongue'.

These points—the use of [ə] in unstressed syllables, the existence of 'weak forms', the disappearance of r in certain positions—had doubtless been established in English for a very long time, but Tucker is one of the earliest writers to admit their existence.[1] He is also, I believe, the first to draw attention to the threefold pronunciation of the plural ending as [s, z, iz], and to explain the circumstances in which each occurs.

There are many more points of interest in *Vocal Sounds*. T. S. Omond says[2] that Tucker 'must always be remembered as one of the first, if not the very first, to apply phonetic method to our verse'. He also held modern views on the pronunciation of Latin. He was aware of the value of phonetic transcription in learning foreign languages; he believed, moreover, that descriptions of contemporary speech sounds would be useful to persons of other times, as well as other places. Phonetic transcription could show coming generations how their predecessors pronounced, 'whereas in our present manner of disguising our language upon paper it would be impossible to conjecture how we sound our words: unless we suppose they will adhere inviolably to our pronunciation, which is an hypothesis not to be admitted'. He wished that 'Tully and Quintilian had been more minute in describing the powers and formation of their letters', and he

---

[1] Jespersen, *M.E.G.*, i, p. 360, states that the earliest Englishman to admit the muteness of r is Walker, in 1775, in a not very specific remark. Tucker is earlier and quite specific.

[2] *English Metrists*, Oxford, 1921, p. 69.

himself is the only person I know to write on phonetics with future phonologists in mind. It is remarkable that he should believe that posterity *would* be interested in the pronunciation of the past; and it is strange that his successors have not consulted him for information on this point.

5

Abraham Tucker believed that another important use for phonetic transcription would be for indicating pronunciation in dictionaries. Compilers 'might after every English word spelt the common way parenthesize the same again in the other characters'. Several adequate systems of transcription for English, besides Tucker's, existed at that time, but none had so far been used for pronouncing dictionaries. William Johnston (1764), James Buchanan (1757 and 1766), and others, had employed various devices—numbers, stress marks, division into syllables, diacritics, differences of fount —in their works, but they had not used phonetic transcription as we understand it. In fact it has been said that the first dictionary to use phonetic respelling was that of Dan Smalley, in 1855;[1] certainly no earlier work is mentioned in bibliographies. However, in 1775 there appeared a dictionary in which the pronunciation was 'parenthesized', just as Tucker had suggested, in a genuine, scientific, phonetic alphabet with seventeen new letters. It was called *The Grand Repository of the English Language*, by Thomas Spence, Teacher of English in Newcastle, and published in that town by T. Saint. It was almost unnoticed at the time, and has escaped attention ever since.

Thomas Spence is a forgotten phonetician, but he is not forgotten as a political thinker, and a good deal is known about his life.[2] He was born in Newcastle-on-Tyne of Scottish parents, very poor, but with a father who gave his children encouragement

---

[1] *American Phonetic Dictionary of the English Language*, Cincinnati. The General Introduction is by A. J. Ellis.

See Bert Emsley, 'Progress in Pronouncing Dictionaries', *American Speech*, vol. xv, p. 55, February 1940; 'The First "Phonetic" Dictionary', *Quarterly Journal of Speech*, vol. xxviii, p. 202, April 1942.

[2] See Olive D. Rudkin, *Thomas Spence and his Connections*, London, 1927.

to read widely. Spence records that when, as a youth, he first
began to study, he found only two subjects in a state of anarchy—
language and politics. Both of these he reduced to order: the one
by a New Alphabet, and the other by a New Constitution.[1] The
two remedies appeared in 1775, the alphabet first. His political
theory was based on the nationalization of land; he proposed
also a five-day week. He was a teacher in Newcastle for some time,
but at the end of 1792 he moved to London, and became a
bookseller in Holborn. He continued there to propagate his
political ideas, which had already got him into some small trouble
in Newcastle; he got into worse trouble in London, and served
seven months' imprisonment in 1794, and another twelve months
in 1799. He died in 1814, and his followers organized themselves
in 1816 into the Society of Spencean Philanthropists, and continued to fall foul of the authorities for some time.

It would be impossible to find a more striking contrast with
the urbane Abraham Tucker than Thomas Spence. 'He was
as poor as any man could well be', wrote a contemporary,[2]
'odd in his manners, perfectly sincere, unpractised in the ways
of the world to an extent few could imagine in a man who had
been pushed about in it as he had been'. His impulsiveness, and
perhaps innocence, is shown by a story of how, one morning, as
he was walking along the streets of London, 'he perceived a very
pretty girl cleaning the steps of a gentleman's house. He stopped,
looked at her, and then enquired if she felt disposed to marry.
On the maid answering in the affirmative, he offered himself,
was accepted, and married the same day.'[3] The marriage was
not a success.

The title-page of his dictionary reads as follows: 'The Grand
Repository of the English Language: containing, Besides the
Excellencies of all other Dictionaries and Grammars of the
English Tongue, the Peculiarity of having the most proper and
agreeable Pronunciation of the alphabetic Words denoted in the

---

[1] *The Important Trial of Thomas Spence*, London, 1803, p. 59.
[2] Francis Place, in a draft of a Memoir of Thomas Spence, B.M. Add. MS.
27808.
[3] Eneas Mackenzie, *Descriptive and Historical Account of Newcastle*, Newcastle, 1827.

most intelligible Manner by a New Alphabet. With a Copper-Plate, Exhibiting the New Alphabet both in Writing and Printing Characters. Intended for the Use of every one whether Native or Foreigner, that would acquire a complete Knowledge of the English Language, with the least Waste of Time and Expence; but especially for those who are but indifferent Readers, from not having been taught to pronounce properly. By Thomas Spence, Teacher of English in Newcastle. Newcastle-upon-Tyne: Printed by T. Saint, for the Author, and sold by him at his School on the Keyside, and by all the Booksellers in Town and Country. MDCCLXXV.'

It is now very rare. The only copy known to me is in the Newcastle Public Library, and I have been able to examine it at my leisure, thanks to the great kindness of the Librarian. The book is duodecimo, $4\frac{1}{2}$ inches by $4\frac{2}{3}$ inches, the pages being badly cropped. It contains 380 unnumbered pages; 348 of these are the dictionary and the rest is a grammar. There are between forty and fifty words to a page, in double columns. The definitions are short but adequate. The stress is marked on the headword by an accent, and the pronunciation in transcription, in capital letters, follows between brackets. Plate III shows a specimen column.[1]

The alphabet contains forty letters, the large number being explained by the fact that each diphthong is represented by a single symbol. 'In reading what is printed in this alphabet', said Spence, 'nothing is required but to sound every letter, and but one way; for each letter represents but one sound, and that invariably in whatever position.' It is of interest that Spence got Thomas Bewick, the famous wood engraver, who was a friend of his, to cut the punches for the types.[2] They bear little sign of that master's hand; in fact, they are unimaginative and clumsy. The book contains an engraved plate, however, which may be the work of Bewick, showing the writing forms of the letters, and these are much pleasanter. This is illustrated in Plate IV. It will be

---

[1] The way the book is bound makes it impossible to reproduce an entire page.
[2] *A Memoir of Thomas Bewick, written by himself.* A new edition, prefaced and annotated by Austin Dobson, Newcastle, 1887, p. 76.

EFF

E'ffort, (EFCRT) n. a ſtruggle; a laborious endeavour.

Effrontery, (EFRINTIRE) n. impudence.

Effulgence, (EFILJINS) n. brightneſs.

Effulgent, (EFILJINT) q. bright; ſhining.

Effuſe, (ɪ.FUZ) v. to pour out; to ſpill.

Effuſion, (EFUꞀIN) n. pouring out.

Effuſive, (EꞀUZIV) q. pouring out.

Eft, (EFT) n a newt; an evet. ad. ſoon.

E. G. an abbreviation for, as for example.

Egg, (EG) n. that which is laid by fowls, from which their young is produced. v. to incite.

E'glantine, (EGLINTIN) n. a ſpecies of roſe.

E'gotiſm, (EGCTIZM) n. too frequent mention of one's ſelf.

E'gotize, (EGOꞀIZ) v. to talk much of one's ſelf.

Egregious, (IGREJIS) q. extraordinary; eminent.

E'greſs, (EGRES) n. the act of going out.

Egreſſion, (EGREꞀIN) n. egreſs.

Eigh, (I) interj. an expreſſion of ſudden delight.

Eight, (AT) q. twice four.

E'ighteen, (ATEN) q. twice nine.

Eighth, (ATꞀ) q. the next in order to the ſeventh.

E'ightieth, (ATEIꞀ) q. the next in order to the ſeventy-ninth.

E'ighty, (ATE) q. eight times ten.

Eigne, (AN) q. the firſt-born; not alienable.

Either, (IꞀIR) pron. one or other. ad. or.

Ejaculate, (IJΛKULAT) v. to dart out: to ſhoot out; to breathe a ſhort occaſional prayer.

PLATE III.—Specimen column from *The Grand Repository of the English Language,* by Thomas Spence, Newcastle-on-Tyne, 1775.

The new Alphabet
in writing and printing Characters.

A a	A a	*H h*	H h	*P p*	P p	*O o*	OO oo
A a	A ä	*I i*	I i	*R r*	R r	*A a*	OU ou
A a	A å	*I i*	I i	*S s*	S s	*A a*	OU ou
A a	AU au	*J j*	J j	*T t*	T t	*b b*	SH sh
B b	B b	*K k*	K k	*U u*	U u	*z z*	ZH zh
D d	D d	*L l*	L l	*U u*	U ŭ	*CH ch*	CH ch
E e	E e	*M m*	M m	*V v*	V v	*H h*	H h
E e	E ě	*N n*	N n	*W w*	W w	*Y y*	TH th
F f	F f	*O o*	O o	*Y y*	Y y	*WH wh*	WH wh
G g	G g	*C c*	C ò	*Z z*	Z z	*X x*	NG ng

EXAMPLES.

We hav a sufibint Insentiv too pirsivir in ar Studez, wen
we konsidir, ŋat too sa, bikez a Hiŋ her not bon ofpklid, yarfor it
kannot be dun, is a Kontridikŋin in Natur; sins yar wuz a ŋrtm
Pereidov Tim wen ŋrre Hizrŋtwez grat ind idmiribl bigun
too be prahusid. In. ert yar wuz a Tim, wen wotovivi zksilicht
hid no Ogzistins.   *Kwintilem.*

It ma hile pirplĕks a karlis Redir ŏv nu Kăriktirz, too disifir ŋi trœ
Sĕns ŋarŏv; ho it ŝhŭd be eze inŭf tœ no it bi a litil Aplikaŝhin ånd
Prăktis.   Ensiklopedea Britănika.

PLATE IV.—Copper-plate from *The Grand Repository.*

noted that the symbol ʒ has its present I.P.A. value. Both upper-
and lower-case forms are provided.

The Grand Repository was intended to make the social advantages
of a correct pronunciation of English available to everyone.
Spence felt strongly about this. 'Why should people be laughed
at all their Lives for betraying their vulgar Education?' he wrote
some years later. 'How ridiculous it is to hear People that can
read saying *Any Think,—A Horange,—Idear,—Noar.*' The best
thing for 'Country People and those who do not keep the best
Company' to do was to 'pay Attention to the Clergy in the Pulpit,
from whom they will have Language which may be depended
upon'.[1] As a matter of fact there is a story that he relied on this
himself: 'When Spence waited upon Mr. Moises, then forenoon
lecturer at All Saints' Church, to ask him to subscribe to his
pronouncing dictionary, the reverend gentleman asked him how
he had attained to a perfection of pronunciation sufficient to
enable him to publish such a work. To this Spence replied, with
more of the world about him than one would have expected:
"Oh, sir, I attend regularly at All Saints' every Sunday forenoon!"'[2]
There are, however, traces of Spence's northern origin in some of
the pronunciations he gives in his dictionary (Francis Place said
that Spence had 'a strong northern burr in his throat'). Most
noticeable is the predominance of the vowel he represents by ĭ,
or Ŧ in its upper-case form, in unstressed syllables. *Sycophant*, e.g. is
rendered sĭkĭfĭnt, *haddock* hădĭk; *haggle* hăgĭl; *swallow* swălĭ.

The Grand Repository is mentioned in the *D.N.B.* article on
Spence, though the writer seems unaware that it is a dictionary.
It is not given in Kennedy's *Bibliography of Writings on the English
Language*. There were several other publications, equally neglected,
in which Spence made use of his alphabet; they are all rare, some
are in the British Museum, some in the Newcastle Public Library,
some have disappeared. Spence was an ardent spelling reformer,
and the first numbers of a periodical called *The Repository of Common
Sense*, consisting of extracts from the best authors in reformed
spelling, had appeared before *The Grand Repository*. I do not know

---

[1] *The Giant Killer, or Anti-Landlord*, No. 1, 6 August 1814.
[2] *Newcastle Magazine*, No. 4, March 1821, p. 427.

for how long it continued: all numbers seem now lost. In 1782 he published *The Real Reading-Made-Easy*, which was described as 'Foreigners' and grown Persons' Pleasing Introductor to Reading English, Whereby all Persons, of whatever Age or Nation, may soon be taught, with Ease and Pleasure, to read the English Language'.

In the same year *A Supplement to the History of Robinson Crusoe*, which expounded some of his political ideas, appeared in two editions, one in ordinary spelling and the other in reformed. Spence wrote in the Preface to the latter (I preserve his spelling; he has abandoned some of his new letters and ligatures, and replaced them by diacritics): 'I hăv prĭntĭd thĭs lĭtĭl Pes ĭn thĭ Kruzoneĭn Mănĭr' (i.e. 'Crusonean Manner', which is how he usually referred to his reformed spelling) 'fŏr thĭ Ez ŏv Fŏrĭnĭrz ănd ŏrdĭnare Redĭrz. I tharfor ădjur aul Krĭtĭks ănd Skŏlĭrz nŏt too ăprĭhĕnd thar Librarez ĭn Danjĭr, ŏr 'thĭngk I ĭntĕnd too kŏmpĕl ithĭr thĕm or thar Chĭldrĭn ĭntoo Kŏnsĭstĕnsez. No, I onle ĭntĕnd too fre thĭ Poor ănd thĭ Stranjĭr, thĭ' Indŭstreŭs ănd thĭ 'Inĭsĭnt frŏm vĕksashŭs, tedeŭs, ănd rĭdĭkĭlĭs 'Absŭrdĭtez. . . . I doo nŏt men ithĭr too hĭndĭr thĭ Prĭntĭng, Redĭng, ŏr ăgreĭbil Kŏntĕmplashĭn ŏv ăne Old Pĕdĭntrez.'

In 1797 Spence apparently started producing a new edition of his dictionary in London, in parts. William Hone (of the *Every-Day Book*) saw some of it, but believed it was never completed.[1] None of it is now to be found.

As early as 1782 Spence was soliciting subscriptions towards printing the Bible in the Crusonean manner. There is no trace of it ever being published, but a corrected proof of seven pages, including the title page, of *The Pronouncing and Foreigners Bible* is in the British Museum.[2] It was printed in London, but bears no date. It had the double purpose of 'establishing an uniform and permanent Manner of Speaking the most sonorous, harmonious, and agreeable English', and was also 'peculiarly calculated to render English universal'. In the Preface he claims that the

---

[1] Letter from Hone to Francis Place, 23 September 1830 (B.M. Add. MS. 27808).

[2] Add. MS. 27808.

Crusonean spelling is particularly suitable for teaching adults, such as Negro slaves or Indian neighbours, to read. 'Moreover there need be no apprehensions that people who are taught only on this Bible . . . will not be able to read those books already extant, for experience has shown the transition to be so easy from the one method to the other, that teaching to read perfectly this New Way first, is found to be the most pleasant and expeditious manner of proceeding, especially if they be adults.'

In 1803 he brought out a full account, under the title of *The Important Trial of Thomas Spence*, of his last trial (which was for publishing and selling, in 1799, a pamphlet called *The Restorer of Society to its Natural State*). There were two editions, one in reformed, the other in normal, spelling. He advises people to take great care of the former edition, for it 'will soon be esteemed a scarce, curious, and valuable book'. The Crusonean manner now shows various concessions to southern usage, particularly in unstressed syllables, and there are other changes in his system, most of them improvements.

Spence is quite well known to students of political theory (he is reputed to be the originator of the phrase 'the Rights of Man'). I believe that study of him would be found rewarding by students of English also.

*   *   *   *

A recent textbook on phonetics mentions 'Sir Henry Sweet' among 'other early writers on the subject'. My witnesses to Professor Firth's thesis—that our antecedents are older and better than we think—have been minor ones, but they are more, I think, than curiosities. Sweet deserved a knighthood as much as anyone, but we should remember that a good three centuries of lively interest in phonetics preceded him.

7

What is a 'letter'?

A better title for this article[1] might, perhaps, be 'what *was* a letter?', for one contention of it is that the word has fairly recently undergone a change, more precisely a *limitation*, in meaning. *Letter* is the key term in any discussion of the relations between speech and writing; but past statements and discussions on this subject are liable now to be misinterpreted, unless this change in meaning is taken into account. Thus J. S. Kenyon has said that John Walker, in his Dictionaries (1791 and later), treats letters 'as the elements of language, with "powers" of sound, as if they were a kind of seed from which the spoken language sprouted and grew'.[2] Walker, certainly, says 'the First principles or Elements of Pronunciation are Letters'; but this is not the naïve remark it seems at first to be, and his use of *letter* by no means implies, as Professor Kenyon suggests, that 'the written form of the language was the language itself'.

It is true that the *Pocket Oxford Dictionary* (1924) defines *letter* as 'any of the symbols of which written words are composed', and this may be taken as a typical definition of modern British and American dictionaries. But the first sense given by Dr Johnson is 'one of the elements of syllables; a character in the alphabet', and it is to be noted about this earlier definition that although the second part of it refers to writing, the first seems to refer to speech. Johnson's illustrative quotations do not clarify further, but it is not necessary to read much in the early English grammarians to realize that this is a real ambiguity. In fact (although there is no

---

[1] I am indebted to Professor J. R. Firth for the original suggestion that I should write this article, and for criticism and advice.

[2] *American Pronunciation* (9th edition, 4th printing, 1946), p. 113.

Published in *Lingua*, Vol. II, 1949.

hint of this in the *O.E.D.*) the strict limitation of the sense of the word to writing is a recent development, and *letter* has, in the past, frequently been used in a sense similar to the modern term *speech-sound*. There can be no doubt that when William Holder (1669) said 'The *Elements* of Language are Letters, viz. Simple discriminations of Breath or Voice',[1] he was not speaking of marks on paper. Equally explicit is John Bulwer's (1648) striking remark that 'Letters the true Elements of Speech [are] made of Motions, nay [are] nothing else but locall motions of the parts of the Mouth.'[2] And there can be no possibility of taking *letter* in its modern sense in Charles Butler's (1633) observation that 'sundry letters, of frequent use in our tongue, have noe peculiar and distinct characters', and his use of the remarkable phrase 'uncharactered letters' to refer to these is surely decisive. Many other instances of this sense of *letter* could be found,[3] and Walker was merely following a common usage.

Latin *litera* was equally ambiguous, and writers in both English and Latin have expressly referred to the double meaning. John Wallis writes in *De Loquela* (1653), p. 2:

> *Litera* dicenda est *Sonus in voce simplex seu incompositus, in simpliciores indivisibilis*. Et peculiari plerumque charactere designatur. Sin malit aliquis non *Sonum* ipsum simplicem, sed Characterem soni simplicis indicem, Literam appellare, fruatur, per me licet, arbitrio suo.[4]

---

[1] A list of the writers from whom illustrations are taken is given at the end of the article.

[2] Compare R. H. Stetson, *Motor Phonetics* (1928): 'Speech is rather a set of movements made audible than a set of sounds produced by movements.'

[3] See, for example, Simon Daines (1640), A. Lane (1700), William Thornton (1793), Edwin Guest (1838). Several writers even use the word *alphabet* in the sense of the *sound-system* of a language.

[4] A translation of *De Loquela* by James Greenwood forms Chapter VIII of his *Essay towards a Practical English Grammar* (1711). The above passage is there rendered:

> A *Letter* may be said to be *a Simple or uncompounded Sound, in a Word, which cannot be divided into any more simple Sounds*. And it is generally marked by a particular Character. But if any would rather have it, that a Letter is not a simple Sound it self, but a *Character* which marks a simple sound; he is at liberty to enjoy his opinion.

And Simon Daines in *Orthoepia Anglicana* (1640), p. 2:

> According to the Etymologie, or strict sense of the term, Letters are
> but certain Characters, or notes, whereby any word is expressed in
> writing: and for this cause were they by the antient Latinists dis-
> tinguished into Letters, as they be Charactericall notes, and Elements,
> as the first grounds or Principles of speech. But this nicety is con-
> founded in the generall acception, which promiscuously terms them
> Letters; and this we shall follow.

Priscian was one of those who distinguished *literae* and *elementa*,
though he draws attention to confusion in their use (and he was
by no means consistent himself):

> Litera igitur est nota elementi et velut imago quaedam vocis literatae,
> quae cognoscitur ex qualitate et quantitate figurae linearum. hoc ergo
> interest inter elementa et literas, quod elementa proprie dicuntur
> ipsae pronuntiationes, notae autem earum literae. abusive tamen et
> elementa pro literis et literae pro elementis vocantur.[1]

Brightland's *Grammar* (1711) criticizes Wallis's definition quoted
above, and insists that 'Letters are the Signs of Sounds, not the
Sounds themselves'; the author, however, himself lapses into
common usage a few pages later when he says 'The several Sorts
of Sounds us'd in Speaking, which we call *Letters* . . .'

There were always, of course, ways of avoiding the ambiguity.
Several synonyms existed for both senses of the word, and *letter*
could be pinned down to one of the two by using for the other
either *character, symbol, note*; or *element, sound, voice*. Both Holder
(1669) and William Thornton (1793) are strict in their use of *letter*
in the spoken sense and *character* in the written, while Hart (1569)
uses *Letter* in the written sense and *voice* in the spoken (an entry in
the index of his *Orthographie* is 'element: of speech, the voice; of
writing the letter'). Wallis, writing in English (1670), said, '*Letters*
are the immediate *Characters* of *Sounds.*' Alternatively, *letter* could
be eschewed altogether; Alexander Hume (*c.* 1617) used *sound* and
symbol, and Robert Robinson (1617) used *sound* and *character*.

---

[1] Institutionum Grammaticarum Libri I-XII ex recensione Martini Hertzii
(Vol. II of Keil's *Grammatici Latini*). Leipzig, 1855.

Edward Search wrote at the beginning of his *Vocal Sounds* (1773):

> I should have entitled my performance letters, but that I should then have been understood of letters written, or characters used upon paper; whereas my intention is to point out the letters spoken, or single sounds composing our syllables and words when we discourse with one another. But these two kinds of letters, the written and the spoken, do not always answer each other.

The word *letter* was, in fact, probably more commonly taken to refer to writing in the late eighteenth century; no established usage arose, however, until in the nineteenth century *speech-sound*, or simply *sound*, was adopted by phoneticians as their principal technical term.[1] And *letter* is not really, even now, limited to the sense of 'written character', in spite of what the dictionaries say:

> Certainly the letter 'h' has not yet yielded up all its mystery. How came it, for example, that the ancient Roman Cockney gratuitously inserted the letter which his modern London fellow improperly omits?

The Times leader[2] from which this is taken was not discussing writing.

Webster's *New International Dictionary* states (s.v. *letter*) 'this confusion of letter with sound is common among early orthoepists. Recent phoneticians avoid this use of letter'.[3] But the fact is that 'this use of letter' is still common enough in circles unfrequented by phoneticians. The latter tend to regard it as merely muddled; it seems possible that it is rather the persistence of what was once a perfectly well-recognized, if perhaps inconvenient, usage, and that in modern dictionaries the community as a whole has had imposed on it a technical limitation of the word *letter* belonging to a small class of people; much as *insect* might be defined to exclude spiders in order to please the zoologists.

---

[1] That it is still very much a technical term is shown by the fact that questions such as 'how many sounds are there in such-and-such a word?' are meaningless to the man in the street.

[2] 16 May 1946.

[3] Curiously enough it omits to explain what 'this confusion' is, and there is nothing to illustrate 'this use of letter'. It is clear. however, that the ambiguity under discussion here is intended.

That there is no record in the *O.E.D.* of what has been a popular usage for centuries is remarkable.

*   *   *

The double sense of *letter* is not only shared with, but, of course, inherited from, *litera*; it is but one sign of the fact that nearly all linguistic thinking in Europe was once in terms of a traditional Latin doctrine which derived, ultimately, from the Greeks. *Litera* was a technical term of this doctrine, of which many other survivals may be found even in contemporary grammatical terminology and classification. A few words about this doctrine will make clear that the word *letter* was used by early English orthoepists, phoneticians, and grammarians in a way which was possibly inconvenient, probably misinterpreted, but certainly not muddled.

Human speech (*vox articulata et literata*), the subject matter of grammar, may, according to this doctrine, be split up into progressively smaller units: sentences, words, syllables and letters. To the study of problems connected with each of these units, one branch of grammar is devoted: syntax, etymology,[1] prosody, and orthography. (This four-fold division can be found in England in nearly all grammars from Aelfric to the end of the eighteenth century, though it is now generally forgotten.) It is the last of these four branches with which we are here concerned. Its name, it should be remarked, was appropriate enough in the days when grammar was a description of Greek in Greek, and little more was involved in it than correct spelling. The name persisted, however, for many centuries after other problems had intruded, in spite of attempts from time to time to supplement or replace it by the term *orthoepy*.[2]

What exactly was this smallest element of language, which formed the object of study of orthography? This can best be answered by considering the most important fact about *litera*:

---

[1] i.e. morphology—a sense different from both the original Stoic, and the present-day meaning of *etymology*.

[2] The heading to one of the sections of John Danes's *Paralipomena Orthographiae* (1638) is 'Orthographia, melius Orthoepia'. Michael Maittaire (1712) gives one of the four parts of grammar as 'Orthoepy, or the Doctrine of Letters'.

that it was a thing with three attributes, *nomen*, *figura*, and *potestas*. *Figura* was the letter as written, *potestas* as pronounced, and by its *nomen* it could be identified for discussion or teaching.

In the time of the Greeks a name was not a necessary attribute of a letter; when a letter did have a name it was, incidentally, the more peculiarly felt as belonging to the letter since it was a foreign borrowing such as *alpha*, *kappa*, with no associations with anything else. By the time the doctrine was fully adapted to Latin, the *nomen* had become an essential feature of all letters, though no longer as distinctive a word as in Greek.

It is not easy to discover the relationship between *figura* and *potestas*. Some grammarians appear to define *litera* as an element of *spoken* language,[1] the written form thus appearing as a secondary thing (compare the Stoic terms στοιχεῖον and χαρακτὴρ τοῦ στοιχείου).[2] It is difficult to avoid the conclusion that for others it was a very sophisticated concept—a structural element of language, with two aspects or realizations, one visible and one audible. Some such concept may be intended by many later writers who seem, on the surface, to be using *letter* in a carelessly ambiguous manner. *Letter* is undoubtedly a structural term for Edwin Guest (1838) when he says 'every vocal [*sc.* voiced] sound has its corresponding whisper sound, that might, if custom had so willed it, have constituted a distinct letter'. He speaks of dividing a word 'into its *literal* elements', and James Elphinston (1790) heads a table of English sounds: 'The Litterary System'.

Normative description, then, of the European vernaculars fell naturally into the terms of this doctrine. Just as Latin had been described within the framework originally designed for Greek, so the phenomena English of were fitted into the framework of Latin rather than investigated impartially. Arguments, for instance, about whether *j* and *v* were letters, continuinlong after g the time

---

[1] e.g. 'vox simplex una figura notabilis' (Victorinus), 'minima pars vocis articulatae' (Donatus). For the principal definitions see L. Jeep, *Zur Geschichte der Lehre von den Redetheilen bei den Lateinischen Grammatikern* (1893), p. 110.

[2] The possible meanings of στοιχεῖον, its relation to γράμμα, and its influence on the meaning of *litera*, are of great interest, but cannot be gone into here. Cp. Ingram Bywater, *Aristotle's Poetics* (1909), p. 262.

when the two figures and the two powers of *i* and *u* had been brought into useful harmony, are only thus explicable; and apparently pointless discussions concerning the status of *h* are only intelligible in the light of the original doctrine.[1]

Neither does speculative thinking on problems of English sounds and spelling, even when it is most adventurous, escape from the terms of the doctrine; it is doubtful, indeed, whether any advantage would result from doing so. An interesting example of this is provided by the numerous attempts there have been to establish some sort of relation between *nomen*, *figura* and *potestas* other than a purely arbitrary one.

Commonest of these is the claim that *nomen* should be related to *potestas* by deriving the former from the latter. Alexander Top (1603) speaks of 'the most improper names of H. and Y.', and Charles Butler (1633) criticizes the name 'dubble u' because it is 'a name of the forme, and not of the force'. There are only ten letters, says William Bullokar (1580), 'whose names and whose sounds rightly agree', and *Right Spelling Very Much Improved* (1704) says, 'Our Letters should have Names, according to their Sound and Force'. The modern 'Phonic' method of teaching reading is based on the same reconciliation of *nomen* and *potestas*, and is remarkably anticipated by Honorat Rambaud (1578) when he says 'lire n'est autre chose que bien nommer les lettres'.

A strange aberration was the reformed spelling of one G. W. (1703) in which the *potestas* was derived from the *nomen*. He gave the letter *h*, for example, the sound [tʃ], and *g* the sound [dʒ]; he then had to invent new symbols for the sounds [h] and [g].[2]

Establishment of a causal relation between *potestas* and *figura* is automatically obtained by the 'visible speech translators' of the Bell Telephone Laboratories, which produce, direct from the

---

[1] That they were not intelligible to A. J. Ellis may be seen from his *Early English Pronunciation*, Part III, p. 805, footnote 3.

[2] See p. 54. It is perhaps interesting to compare with this the fact that in London costermongers' 'back slang' the *nomen* of *h*, and not its *potestas*, is used to produce the word for 'half': *flatch* (though speakers of this mid-nineteenth-century slang were supposed to have been illiterate).

spoken word, sound 'spectrograms' which are legible.[1] But before this brilliant discovery many attempts had been made to derive the *figura* from the *potestas*.

John Wilkins (1668) said 'there should be some kind of sutableness, or correspondency of the figures to the nature and kind of the Letters which they express'; and it is for his 'Visible Speech' (1864) that A. M. Bell is chiefly remembered. But before Bell, Wilkins had exhibited his own suggestions for what he calls 'a *Naturall Character* of the Letters', departing altogether from the Roman alphabet, on p. 379 of his *Essay*; and Messrs. Holdsworth and Aldridge of the Bank of England had published in 1766 a shorthand the characters of which were derived from the same principle. Sir William Jones (1786) held a theory concerning the letters of all alphabets, 'which at first, probably, were only rude outlines of the different organs of speech', which was anticipated by van Helmont's theories concerning the Hebrew alphabet in 1657.

Less extreme are those alphabets which do not aim at being entirely 'representational', but assign symbols of similar shape to related sounds. This is done by Francis Lodwick (1686), 'the more regularly to sort them into Classes, and to express the derivation of Letters of the same Organe, the one from the other'. The *Alphabet Universel* of Emile Fourner (1861) is based on a similar principle, and so were the early phonotypic alphabets of Isaac Pitman (1842) and the Organic Alphabet of Paul Passy and Daniel Jones. It is noteworthy that one of the principles of the International Phonetic Association enunciated in 1888 is that 'the new letters should be suggestive of the sounds they represent, by their resemblance to the old ones'.

The traditional approach to speech sounds and spelling had all the defects of a dogma, and did not conduce, on the whole, to very much original thinking. Its effects are only too obvious, as William Holder said, 'in the writings of some Learned men, who coming to treat of the nature of Letters, speak of them by Tradition, as of

---

[1] See Ralph K. Potter, 'Visible Patterns of Sound', *Science*, 9 November 1945; R. K. Potter, G. A. Kopp, and H. C. Green, *Visible Speech*, New York, 1947.

some remote exotick thing, whereof we had no knowledge, but by uncertain and fabulous relations'; and it led to absurb statements such as that of the usually acute thinker, James Howell (1662), that Spanish *oveja* is a remarkable word because it contains all five vowels! 'The powers of the letters', says H. C. Wyld, perhaps a little harshly, 'is a phrase we get positively sick of in the seventeenth century.'[1]

Students of linguistics are probably better off without the ambiguous word *letter*.[2] Typographical discussions concerning *figura*, and phonological arguments concerning *potestas*, are still the main preoccupation of theorists of phonetic transcription today, but such problems are perhaps more easily handled in terms of *speech-sound*, *symbol*, and *phoneme*.[3] It may, however, be questioned whether, if *letter* had been retained in something like its traditional functional sense, the need for a phoneme theory would ever have arisen—though we should, certainly, have subtle theories of the *letter* in its place.

The following is a list of the works mentioned above. Unless stated otherwise, the place of publication is London.

Brightland, John. *A Grammar of the English Tongue*, 1711.

Bullokar, William. *Booke at large, for the Amendment of Orthographie for English speech . . .*, 1580.

Bulwer, John. *Philocophus: or the Deafe and Dumbe Mans Friend*, 1648.

Butler, Charles. *The English Grammar*, Oxford, 1633.

Daines, Simon. *Orthoepia Anglicana*, 1640.

Danes, John. *Paralipomena Orthographiae*, 1638.

Elphinston, James. *Inglish Orthography Epittomized*, 1790.

Fourner, Emile. *L'Alphabet Universel Déduit du Mécanisme de la Parole*, Paris, 1861.

---

[1] *History of Modern Colloquial English*, 3rd edition, p. 117.

[2] Though Louis Hjelmslev considers 'es war ganz sicher nicht als ein Fortschritt anzusehen, wenn man nach dem Einzug der Phonetik in die Sprachwissenschaft den Terminus "Laut" statt "Buchstabe" einführte'. ('Uber die Beziehung der Phonetik zur Sprachwissenschaft', *Archiv. für vergleichende Phonetik*, Band II, Heft 3, July 1938.)

[3] See J. R. Firth, 'The Technique of Semantics', *Trans. Phil. Soc.*, 1935, pp. 55 and 56, especially footnote.

Greenwood, James. *An Essay towards a Practical English Grammar*, 1711.

Guest, Edwin. *A History of English Rhythms*, 1838. Edited by W. W. Skeat, 1882.

Hart, John. *An Orthographie* . . ., 1569.

van Helmont, F. M. B. *Alphabeti vere Naturalis Hebraici brevissima Delineato*, Sulzbach, 1657.

Holder, William. *Elements of Speech*, 1669.

Holdsworth, William and Aldridge, William. *Natural Shorthand*, 1766.

Howell, James. *A new English Grammar*, 1662.

Hume, Alexander. *Of the Orthography and Congruitie of the Britan Tongue.* Edited by Henry B. Wheatley, 1865. (Probably written about 1617.)

Jones, Sir William. 'Discourse on the Hindus, delivered 2d of February, 1786.' *Works*, Vol. I, 1799.

Lane, A. *A key to the Art of Letters*, 1700.

Lodwick, Francis. 'An Essay Towards an Universal Alphabet.' *Philosophical Transactions*, Vol. XVI, p. 126, 1686.

Maittaire, Michael. *The English Grammar*, 1712.

Passy, Paul, and Jones, Daniel. 'Alphabet Organique.' *Le Maître Phonétique*, Bourg-la-Reine, France, 1907.

Pitman, Sir Isaac. *The Phonographic Journal*, Vol. I, *passim*, 1842.

Rambaud, Honorat. *La Declaration des Abus que lon commet en escriuant* . . ., Lyons, France, 1578.

Right Spelling Very much Improved, 1704.

Robinson, Robert. *The Art of Pronuntiation*, 1617.

Search, Edward (pseud., i.e. Abraham Tucker). *Vocal Sounds*, 1773.

Thornton, William. *Cadmus*, Philadelphia, U.S.A., 1793.

Top, Alexander. *The Oliue Leafe*, 1603.

W., G. *Magazine, Or, Animadversions on the English Spelling*, 1703.

Wallis, John. *De Loquela*, Oxford, 1653.

Wallis, John. 'Two persons Deaf and Dumb taught to speak and to Understand a Language.' *Philosophical Transactions*, Vol. V, p. 1087, 1670.

Wilkins, John. *An Essay towards a Real Character*, 1668.

8

Writing systems

I want to discuss in this paper what actually happens when we set out to represent language, which is primarily a spoken thing, in signs which our eyes, instead of our ears, are to interpret. Writing seems such a very natural thing to us, who are fortunate enough to be literate, that it is difficult to approach it objectively to see how it really does work; a scientific approach to writing is, in fact, of very recent date. The traditional methods of writing which are found all over the world are the result of a slow evolution of many thousands of years. No conscious theorizing went to their construction, as far as we can tell; nobody sat down to think out what principles should govern the invention and application of systems of writing, what were the things to aim for and the things to avoid, what it was possible to do and impossible to do. Nevertheless, the method of trial and error, given time enough to work itself out, usually brings the results needed, and the elimination of devices which it was found did not work properly, and the further cultivation of devices which were successful, led finally to that extraordinarily ingenious invention, alphabetic writing, the basis of a very large part of human civilization.

Nowadays, however, we require methods of visual symbolization of speech for many more different purposes than we did in the past. The teaching of modern languages has become of great importance, and to be efficiently carried out it demands the use of phonetic transcriptions; hitherto illiterate people all over the

Paper given, under the title 'The Visual Symbolization of Speech', to the International Shorthand Congress, London, in July 1937. A version of the paper was published in the *Reprint of Papers and President's Address*, London, 1938, and also in *Pitman's Business Education*, Vol. IV, 1937.

world, brought into contact with modern civilization, require new
alphabets to reduce their unwritten languages to permanent
form; and lastly, of particular interest to us here, the speeding up
of modern life makes systems of shorthand a necessity. For all
these purposes we cannot allow the method of trial and error to
take its own time in working out practical solutions. We cannot
rely on lucky accidents any longer, but must tackle the problems
scientifically. Thus it was that about a century or more ago
a number of people in various places set out to try to discover
what the principles and theories of writing, which had been
followed unconsciously in the past, really were. The problem of
how to represent speech visually in the most satisfactory manner
played a large part in giving rise to the science of phonetics.
The problem is still one of its main concerns, though it now has
many others. I want here to give a brief account of what phonetics
has to say on the problem, and in particular how it applies to
shorthand construction.

The first thing to notice is what appears at first sight to be the
complete irreconcilability of the two modes of communication,
the oral and the written. We cannot give a *picture* of speech by
marks on paper; when we say that writing represents speech,
we do not use 'represent' in the same sense as when we say a
picture represents a landscape, but rather as when we say a cross
on a map represents a church. This is obvious enough; but it is
very apt to be forgotten. Neglect of this fundamental principle
has given rise to many fruitless arguments, though it is true that
it has caused little serious damage except frayed tempers, lost
time, and the invention of a few useless methods of shorthand
and phonetic transcription.

What are the elements to which we give our visual symbols?
People are not always clear on this point, and systems of writing
are often classified according to the different things that the
symbols they employ are supposed to stand for: words, syllables,
or speech-sounds. But this is not really the best way of looking at
it. *All* systems of writing known to us give their symbols to words;
the differences between them lie in the way these symbols are
constructed. They may be simple symbols, or they may be made

up from a small number of subsidiary signs; but however they are made up, it must not be forgotten that they will be read as words, and probably written as words also. In the process of *learning* any system of writing, one is, of course, conscious of the smaller elements which go to make up the complex word symbols; but the ordinary literate human being, reading naturally, pays no attention to individual letters. It is the shape of the word as a whole which his eye attends to. Were this not so, reading would be an impossibly laborious process. Those who write shorthand know also that it is impossible to attain any speed unless word symbols— 'outlines'—are written straight off, without analysis into the elements into which they were divided when they were learnt. Briefly, then, the object of writing is to provide an unambiguous symbol for every word in the language concerned.

It is possible to give each word a completely different symbol, which is what is done in Chinese writing. Very many different symbols are needed by such a system. Once they are learnt they can be managed simply enough—an educated Chinese reads as easily as, and possibly more quickly than, an educated Englishman —but the labour of learning them is considerable.

However, the number of symbols needed can be reduced by a process of analysis of the various words contained in the language. This is a complicated business involving many difficult problems, most of which, however, need not detain us here. The word is just as much a unit of speaking—or hearing—as of reading or writing. It is innervated from the brain as a whole, and the unpractised person finds it extremely hard to isolate any one part of a word from the rest. But if, by means of an analysis which is really artificial in the extreme, we do succeed in splitting up the various words of a language, we shall find that similar bits of sound (or of muscular movement—it depends on which way we are looking at it) tend to recur. It must not be thought that these similar bits are elements from which the speaker builds up the words he pronounces; that, psychologically, would be quite a wrong point of view. But the similarities are there, nevertheless; every language employs a limited number only of types of movement of the vocal organs.

We can, then, isolate and identify, quite arbitrarily, these bits
of sound, to which it will be convenient to give the name *isolates*
(a term borrowed from the mathematician, H. Levy[1]). If we give
each isolate a distinctive sign, we can build up a symbol for each
word according to the analysis we have made of it.

So far so good; but here the real problems start. They arise
out of two different things: the degree to which we split up our
words, the number of different parts we divide them up into,
that is to say the *size* of the isolates; and the degree of similarity
which we shall consider sufficient to enable any two bits of words
to be identified, that is to say the *generality* of the isolates (for the
bits of words are only similar; they are never, and could not in
the nature of things be, identical).

Examples will make both these points clearer. Consider the
English word *father*. If English was an unwritten language, we
could divide the word into two isolates, *fa-ther*, allot a sign to
each isolate, and produce a symbol for the word by placing these
two signs together. This would be a syllabic writing system, and
if we followed it out in English we should find ourselves saddled
with an unwieldy number of different signs; it is a system quite
unsuited to the structure of the language. Japanese, on the other
hand, can analyse all its words into about fifty different syllabic
isolates, and it can obtain on this basis quite a convenient system
of writing. In English, and languages which are like English in
structure, we shall find ourselves better off if we take smaller
isolates, that is to say if we divide each word into smaller parts
than syllables. We could, for example, split up *father* into four
bits: *f-a-th-er*, and give a sign to each of these isolates. We shall
then have to make our word-symbol from four subsidiary signs
instead of two, but the total number of signs required to write the
language, following this method, will be much less. An analysis
into smaller isolates than syllables results in alphabetic writing,
but in alphabetic writing variation in the size of the isolates is still
possible. We can split up *choose* into three parts: *ch-oo-se*, or into
four: *t-sh-oo-se*. *Steps* can be divided as *st-e-ps* or *s-t-e-p-s*. Chance

---

[1] See, for instance, *The Universe of Science* (London, 1932).

7

has played a part in the size of the isolates taken by existing methods of writing; in Russian, for example, quite a large isolate, *shtsh*, is given one single sign. Practice has shown that the smaller the isolates resulting from our analysis, the fewer the number of signs required to write the language will be, from Chinese, which takes entire words as isolates, to a modern phonetic 'broad' transcription, which takes the smallest elements it can.

The first point, then, where different kinds of analysis are possible, is in the size of the isolates taken. Difference is also possible in the generality of the isolates. When we are making a 'broad' phonetic transcription of English, for example, we would divide a word such as *little* into four parts: *l-i-tt-le*. The first part and the last part have easily distinguishable sounds, but practice shows that if they are given the same sign, if they are, that is to say, taken as the same isolate, no ambiguity will result. In the same way we can identify the initial consonants of the two words *key* and *cow*, where the difference is smaller but nevertheless apparent. Our aim, it must be remembered, is to provide an unmistakable symbol for each word, and the amount of similarity between bits of words sufficient for them to be given the same sign depends on whether unambiguous word symbols will result. When this has been attained we can make further distinctions if anything should make it advisable to do so. It is a point of interest that there would probably be no confusion between any words in English if we wrote the first sound and the last sound of the word *hang* with the same sign; there is such great difference between the two, however, that it is worth while distinguishing them.

Japanese and the Semitic languages both provide examples of syllabic writing, but there is a difference between them in the generality of the isolates taken: those of the latter are more general than those of the former, in that they ignore the vowel quality of the syllable. For example, *ka* and *ki* would be written with the same sign in Hebrew, with different signs in Japanese. (It became necessary in Semitic writing systems to introduce vowel pointing, or diacritics to the syllable, when ambiguities had to be guarded against.)

When we leave naturally evolved methods of writing, and come to consciously invented systems of modern times, we find another important principle which it is well to observe. This is that the kind of analysis we make—the size and generality of our isolates—ought to depend not only on the structure of the language but also on the purpose to which we are going to put the writing. The kind of analysis suited to one purpose will not necessarily be the best for another. If, for example, we want to work out a rational orthography for English, we should try to use as few signs as possible consistent with the resulting word-symbols being unambiguous. We want a system which can be easily learnt by children and easily handled by printers. The quicker it can be written the better, but we are not aiming primarily at speed. If, however, we are constructing an English shorthand, then speed obviously must be the first consideration. We do not expect a shorthand to be easy to learn (though, of course, it must not be too difficult), and we can leave printers to deal with it as best they can. Our analysis of the language for shorthand will not, therefore, be made with a view to discovering the minimum number of symbols required, and it is in practice found that a combination of all the different types of analysis will give the greatest speed. Every kind of isolate can be found in a well-constructed shorthand. Arbitraries or grammalogues are like the symbols of Chinese writing: the entire word (sometimes even the phrase or sentence) is the isolate. In most modern systems the beginning part—the part before the vowel—of words like *strip*, *clear*, *try*, *Spain*, *choose*, are all equally regarded as single isolates, and given one sign each. Writing without vowel points is very much the same as the Semitic kind of syllabary, and the sign) in Pitman shorthand is a good example of a very general syllabic isolate, since at the beginning of a word it stands for any vowel plus *s*.

Writing is not an end in itself, and we need systems of writing not as beautiful or as true as possible, but as well fitted as we can get them to the purpose for which they are required. When constructing any system of visual symbolization of speech, convenience must in the long run be the only guide, and practice, not abstract logical principles, the only valid test.

9
Isaac Pitman
1

Although language is a most important function of man, and might without exaggeration be said to be the basis of all human co-operation, it has been the subject of remarkably little scientific investigation. At first sight it might appear strange that, while most other processes vital to the individual's survival (though still perhaps mysteries to the majority) have always been the subject of experts' study, the body of scientific linguistic knowledge goes back only perhaps a hundred years or a little more. And yet language is no less vital to the survival of all social groupings.

The reason is that language has worked satisfactorily enough for practical purposes; there has been far less incentive to investigate its mechanisms than those of a more fallible function such as digestion. The ordinary man is content to use his faculty of speech, and, if he is literate, his power of writing, in the highly skilled manner made natural to him by his upbringing, without for a moment wondering how these two facilities work, or whether he is obtaining the maximum efficiency from them. An occasional hitch in the smooth working of his language—an anomaly in spelling, or difficulty in listening to an unfamiliar pronunciation—may raise a suspicion that there are problems somewhere; but these are usually hitches only, easily overcome. He is never faced with a complete breakdown, and the absence of urgent need to look for radical solutions has, up to now, made even the formulation of problems unnecessary. Language is, of course, as much a source of interest and pride as any other human bodily function; but the

Published as a separate pamphlet, with the full title *Isaac Pitman: a Pioneer in the Scientific Study of Language*, and a Foreword by the late Arthur Lloyd James, by Sir Isaac Pitman and Sons, Ltd., London, in 1937. It is reprinted here with a few omissions.

ordinary man's interest is superficial and spasmodic, and his knowledge and theories of means of communication are haphazard and whimsical.

The specialist in linguistic matters has been equally affected by the remarkable efficiency of language, and its consequent unquestioned acceptance. Nearly all language study has been of the 'philological' kind—what Sir Richard Paget has called the *botany* of language. An immense amount of work has been done in classification, the establishment of texts, the working out of relationships, and so on—work which should not in any way be belittled. But none of this work has involved that consideration of more fundamental problems which is necessary if *conscious control* of language is to be obtained, for the simple reason that little or no need for control has made itself apparent.

Certain developments in our civilization, however, seem to be changing this state of affairs, and hitches in communication are becoming more and more difficult to surmount. Ambiguities in vocabulary which formerly led only to interminable arguments of philosophers can now cause serious trouble and even international incidents; the presentation of modern scientific theories and discoveries is frequently seriously handicapped by purely linguistic factors; the new importance of the spoken word in radio, the telephone, and sound films has found our ordinary technique of speech inadequate; modern advertising and propaganda methods are making an examination of the 'emotive' function of language necessary both for those who use them and those on whom they are used. We are beginning to realize, in fact, that language is no longer as efficient as it might be for the many different ends it now has to serve; and, in response to this, linguistic investigation is ceasing to be predominantly philological, or the favourite playground of amateurs, and becoming a science essential to human welfare. Botany is not enough. Scientific research is as essential to the future development of language as are the investigations of Rothamsted and Aberystwyth to the future of agriculture.

The various publications of Ogden and Richards, the philosophical ideas of Carnap and the Vienna Circle, reformed methods of teaching foreign languages—even Latin and Greek—are examples from only a few of the widely differing fields where profounder questioning into speech is spreading. Our concern here is with a small, but nevertheless important, part of this linguistic activity—the symbolization of speech by visual signs. The science of phonetics is nowadays a discipline of numerous practical applications, and one of its primary objects is the investigation of how the vocal organs work when producing speech. Broadly speaking, however, phonetics arose out of the anomalies and difficulties of the English system of spelling, and its first examinations of speech mechanism were made solely as a means to the working out of a more rational method of writing. It was, in fact, the first sign in modern times of a critical interest in language with a view to conscious control of it; and although other more urgent problems of communication have arisen, this first concern of phonetics, the study of the visual representation of speech, remains of first-rate importance, on which much work is still to be done. It is the purpose of this essay 'to show the part played, in the early and vital stages of this study, by a man whose contribution to science is as much neglected as his name is well known. Success in business is not commonly held to be compatible with scholarship; the prominence attained by the stenographic side of Sir Isaac Pitman's work in the world of commerce has obscured the value of the basic principles on which this stenography was based, and his careful examination of, and consequent attempts to reform, writing in general.

2

In 1832 Isaac Pitman, who was just nineteen years of age and had previously been working as a clerk for his father, obtained his first post as a schoolmaster. Here he very soon became aware of certain problems, at that time beginning to make themselves increasingly evident, in methods of representing speech by visual symbols. The most striking one, though not the first to engage his attention, was connected with the ordinary spelling of English. Peculiarities and vagaries had already been present in our spelling for some centuries, but whereas in the past the fortunate few who were able to read and write had, for the most part, sufficient leisure to assimilate these peculiarities, and had even come to look upon them with affection and pride, with the growth of popular education and the spread of literacy these anomalies began to be felt as a serious nuisance. Alphabetic writing is the result of a long evolution of methods of speech symbolization, worked out more or less by a process of trial and error. It can be a highly efficient means of writing, and it has, at different times and in different places, been employed to its fullest advantage; but it is not put to its best use in the writing of English. Five or six hundred years ago ours was an alphabetic system which, though not ideal, must have been reasonably easy to handle for the few who made use of it. Since that time, however, English pronunciation has undergone profound changes, while the spelling has altered hardly at all; where there have been modifications, they have mostly been due to the mistaken and pedantic notion that spelling should illustrate the etymology of a word, and consequently have only been for the worse. The confusion that has resulted is sufficiently apparent, and there is no need to illustrate it here by bringing forward the many anomalous series of words of the *plough, rough, through, though* type. An enthusiastic young teacher, working, as Isaac Pitman was, for one of the pioneer voluntary education organizations, and dealing with children from quite unlettered families, must have bitterly resented the disproportionate amount of time which had to be spent, before education proper could really begin, on the painful process of learning to read and write.

A rather different problem of speech symbolization, less striking and urgent, was at the same time beginning to occupy many people's attention. This also, like the problem of our traditional spelling, can, not too fancifully, be linked with social changes taking place in the country. It does not appear impossible that there should be some connexion between the gradual speeding up of life then taking place, especially in commerce, and the increasing interest in shorthand. Since 1558, when stenography was 'rediscovered' in England, numbers of scholars had devoted their time to the subject, and the highest point of their researches was reached, at the end of the eighteenth century, with the works of

Gurney, Byrom, Blanchard and Taylor. Considerable speed could be attained by writers of these four systems; they were, however, fairly difficult to learn, and it seemed from the principles on which they were based that no further advance in the direction they were taking was possible. The beginning of last century saw a growing demand for a system of stenography which could be moderately easily learnt, without demanding the intelligence and training of a scholar, and suitable for the use, among other things, of rapidly expanding commerce.

Isaac Pitman was the more readily made aware of these problems since he had already, from an early age, taken an interest in pronunciation and other questions of language. He had studied the *Principles of English Pronunciation* prefixed to John Walker's famous Pronouncing Dictionary, in which he had also verified the pronunciation of every word which he suspected of being an anomaly. He had learnt to write Taylor's method of shorthand, and was engaged in teaching it to his pupils. He was, in addition, a man of tireless industry and application; he had already undertaken, and nearly completed, the gigantic task of collating the references in Bagster's Comprehensive Bible, a task which demanded all he had of these qualities for almost three years. Nobody, in fact, could have been better fitted to undertake the exhaustive examination of speech symbolization to which he devoted the rest of his life. Before passing, however, to a detailed consideration of his work and discoveries, it would be as well to explain briefly the basic principles of sound notation, and also to mention some of those difficulties and prejudices which always appear when considering questions of speech, and might possibly influence the reader in his estimation of Isaac Pitman's work.

3

There are some prejudices, common to all sides of language, which lie very deep in human nature, and arise from causes not all of which have been explained. It is a fact, which can easily be verified, that many people—perhaps all who have not become aware of the subtle influence of these prejudices—find it impossible to treat linguistic questions in the light of reason alone. The reader may have noticed how surprisingly short tempers can become in all discussions on language; with what resentment the most harmless observations on a person's speech behaviour are often met; how opinions on the subject of speech are often held with a pugnacity hardly merited by their importance or the evidence supporting them. It is unnecessary to attempt either to explain or dispel these deep-seated prejudices in the course of this essay; but the reader must be on his guard against all judgements—his own or anyone else's—on questions of language, in which something more than consideration of the facts seems to intrude. It is usually prudent to treat appeals to preserve the 'purity' of a language, invocations of 'correctness', and signs of hostility to innovations, as at least suspect when they appear in argument. While Isaac Pitman himself was very largely free from the influence of these irrational prejudices, he was to come across them in others, in the course of his attempts to propagate his ideas, only too frequently.

Whatever the nature and origin of these prejudices, they form the first, and a very serious, barrier to the objective analysis of language. When they have been overcome, other difficulties, arising out of the nature itself of the subject matter of our investigation, still remain to be negotiated. The very closeness of our speech to us is a difficulty; reading, speaking and writing are so very natural, so much a part of our normal life, and so bound up with all we do and everything around us, that it is hard to attain that objective distance from which they can be seen in true perspective. Language has to be isolated for examination, and it may so easily be changed in the process of isolation without our suspecting the fact. All forms of human behaviour are difficult to get under the microscope, and language is the most complex and delicate of all.

These are difficulties which have to be faced by every scientific investigator of language. There are others which are found only in the special problems we are here concerned with. Research into the relations between speech and writing is complicated by the fact that, for all literates, the two forms of communication are so closely associated that knowledge of one may unwittingly influence consideration of the other. It is an elementary, but often forgotten, fact that speech is primary. Men spoke before they wrote, and, indeed, the majority of the population of the world still possess only the oral form of communication with their fellow creatures. However much independence any written form of language may have won for itself, it is in the end only a secondary production, and must ultimately depend for its validity on the spoken word. This should be self-evident, but it is neglected more often than one would think by those who discuss the subject. The explanation is that writing, until very recently, has been the monopoly of a privileged few. It was an object of mystery for those not in a position to acquire it, and those who were masters of its secrets were tempted to think that they alone possessed the true form of language. Both the spread of literacy, involving the disappearance of its monopoly character, and the increasing importance given to speech by modern inventions, are rapidly destroying the prestige which writing has so long enjoyed; but many signs of unnatural reverence for it linger on. We have passed the stage when the simple reduction of a wish or curse to written form was sufficient to give it magical potency; or when the peculiarity of Semitic script, which is written from right to left, was thought a sufficient explanation of why supposedly cognate words were pronounced back to front in English. Theories, however, are still put forward on the subject of language which depend, usually implicitly, on the assumption that writing is its real or most important form; and the spelling of words is often taken as a criterion of their pronunciation. Opposition to spelling reform is in large measure resistance to what is felt as an attack upon the sacredness of our orthography.

We, in these days, with a century of experience behind us, are prepared for difficulties and prejudices of this kind; we know where to look for them and when they are likely to intrude. But from those who first tackled these and similar problems, remarkable clarity and independence of mind must have been required; and there is no better example among them of this clarity and independence than Sir Isaac Pitman.

4

The principles involved in the representation of speech by writing are few and simple. It must first of all be remembered that visual symbols only represent noises *by convention*. Our written symbols must be purely arbitrary, and associations between them and the noises we are representing have to be established by education. This means that we must be careful with the adjectives we apply to any system of writing; if we use words like 'true', 'accurate', 'correct', we shall confuse ourselves unless we bear in mind that 'convenient' is really what we mean. Traditional English spelling is to be criticized, not because it gives a false picture of reality, but because the conventions necessary to its use are complex, irregular and cumbersome.

In actual fact, however, it is not any specific vocal utterance to which we give our arbitrary symbols. What we need is a visual means of communication which, although it must depend ultimately on the spoken language, shall be independent of specific concrete speech acts, and capable of manipulation by itself. The process of analysis and abstraction by which men arrived at that deceptively simple fiction, the 'word', is one which need not be discussed here. It is enough to say that without these fictions we should be quite unable to write, for it is to words that we allot our visual symbols. It is important to remember that our signs are, therefore, signs for abstractions, and not for concrete physical entities.

The first stage of every primitive system of writing was to give one single separate sign to each word. Chinese alone still follows this practice; every other script has advanced to a more practicable method. Writing by means of so-called 'ideograms' (not a very fortunate name for them) has many serious defects, the chief being the obvious difficulty of elaborating, learning and remembering sufficient distinctive signs. We do not know how, or by whom, the brilliant solution to these difficulties was arrived at; like every other stroke of genius, it is simplicity itself, though far from easy to explain in moderately non-technical language. The basis of writing is the provision of a distinctive symbol for every word; but whereas the word-symbols of ideographic writing are simple, all other methods are based on complex word-symbols, just as distinctive as ideograms, but built up from a small number of elementary signs. It is in the way in which these elementary signs are put together that the real ingenuity of writing, as we know it, lies. A 'word' is an abstraction constructed from a series of similar vocal utterances, and as an abstraction it cannot, of course, be subject to any physical analysis; it is, however, possible to make an acoustic analysis of a single utterance, taken as typical, of a word. If a series of aural sensations representing a large number of different words is analysed, and the resulting elements, or units, compared, some of these units will be found to resemble others—one part of one word will be similar to part of another. Practice has shown that if signs are given to each group of similar units, the analysed words can then be re-made, as it were, on paper, and unambiguous symbols obtained for them.

It must not be forgotten that, even in constructing the most exacting notation, analysis of a physical act of speech is only made to provide a convenient symbol for an abstraction; we can never try to represent in writing this one single act. This means that we can take liberties with our analysis wherever we feel it to our advantage, and we need only be governed by the principle that whatever in practice works conveniently and simply is justifiable.

Naturally, these principles of writing were not consciously applied in the course of its development from the primitive ideographic state to modern alphabets. Trial and error, success in practice, kept people to them. But their clear understanding is essential in modern times for anyone who wishes to work out new methods of writing, particularly shorthand and phonetic transcription. It was only by the rational application of these principles that Isaac Pitman was able to raise shorthand construction to an entirely new level and make real advance in the art possible.

5

By a fortunate combination of circumstances, which need not detain us here, Isaac Pitman did not have to wait long to put his theoretical interest in these matters to practical use, for he was invited, early in 1837, to invent and prepare for publication a new system of shorthand. By September of that year he had it fully worked out and was using it himself, and on 15 November it was put on sale in the form of a small fourpenny pamphlet.

It is not intended to discuss the merits of this new system from the technical stenographic point of view. Questions concerning the use of devices such as thickening, halving, position, and the geometric basis, can be left to the professional shorthand writer to settle by experience; the present position of the Pitman system leaves little doubt as to what the answer will be. Nor are we concerned with the various modifications introduced by the author during his lifetime. Our interest lies in the guiding idea behind the system, and the fundamentals of its construction; these were present from the beginning, and are of equal value whatever kind of visual signs are used to give them expression.

As mentioned above, none of the numerous systems of shorthand then in existence was capable of any further development owing to the very basis of their construction. They all rested on the traditional English spelling; that is to say they started from an analysis of the language which had been made—or rather evolved —with a different purpose in view, which corresponded to a much earlier stage of the spoken language, and which was so inconsistently applied that the word-symbols constructed from it were little better than ideograms. True, most of the systems contained instructions to the learner to pay attention to the sounds of the words transcribed, but this meant little more than leaving out silent consonants and occasionally simplifying unnecessarily complicated combinations of letters.

The revolutionary basis of the new Pitman system was that it started from an entirely new *ad hoc* analysis of the language. The idea was so simple that, once hit on, it seemed natural and inevitable to everyone, and little credit has been given to Pitman for it. Many who have since advocated other systems and criticized Phonography, as the new system was called, failed entirely to realize that their own rival systems had adopted intact Pitman's basic ideas.

Not only did Pitman make the far-reaching discovery that any advance in stenography required a completely new analysis of the language, but he realized quite clearly that this analysis must be made with the purpose of stenography in view; that is to say that while the aim of ordinary writing is to provide clear, simple word-symbols, easy to handle and construct, for shorthand the emphasis is not on the simplicity of the word-symbol but on the speed with which it can be written.

The analysis from which the word symbol is built up, then, need not necessarily be made with a view to discovering the minimum number of characters required. This is where Pitman made his second great discovery. He saw that a less minute analysis would involve the provision of a greater number of characters, but that this would easily be compensated for by the rapidity with which the resulting outlines could be written. That is to say, 'lumps' of sound, which longhand would split up in order to reduce the number of its signs, could, in constructing shorthand word-symbols, be allowed to remain as units to which single characters are attached. An example will make this clearer. For traditional English orthography the following words: *say*, *ray*, *Tay*, *stay*, *tray*, *stray*, putting the vowel on one side, contain in all three different consonant elements only. Pitman saw that, instead of taking the last three words as being composed of elements which have already occurred in the first three, he had just as much right to look upon the six words as containing six different elements. This entails six different signs in order to write the words, as against the three of longhand (vowels always excluded); but the gain in speed is obvious:

> *say*

> *ray*

> *Tay*

> *stay*

> *tray*

> *stray*

It is worth noting that, more by accident than design, traditional

English orthography in two cases leaves as a single unit a 'lump' of sound that it could have analysed further. It would be quite possible (without much gain in convenience) to split up *ch* as in *cheese*, and *j* as in *jam*, into *t* plus *sh*, and *d* plus *zh*, respectively, as is done in modern phonetic transcriptions. Pitman's extension of this, in the way I have shown, demanded the provision of well over a hundred characters for Phonography, as against the twenty-six of our alphabet; but meant at the same time, once the characters are learnt,[1] tremendous economy of effort in writing.

The next point of originality was in the treatment of vowels. Taylor's system, the one which Isaac Pitman first learnt, was one in which the vowels were disjoined, not incorporated in the outline. Pitman followed this practice and was able to turn it to great advantage, for, as can easily be demonstrated, English is a language of consonants. The abbreviations of the London Telephone Directory, *gngrcr*,[2] for example, are clear to everyone, and it can be found by experiment that in talking very little differentiation between vowels is needed for intelligibility. Let the reader try saying aloud the first sentence of this paragraph to a friend, substituting the so-called obscure or neutral vowel for all the other vowels:

ther nerxt pernt erv errergernerlerter werz ern . . .

and he will be perfectly intelligible.

Hence Pitman confined the real outlines of his words to consonants only. A highly ingenious arrangement of vowel points, based on the acoustic properties of the sounds and not, as in every other previous system, on their order in the alphabet, was provided, and by their means any vowel can be indicated with precision where necessary. In practice, however, when sufficient familiarity is obtained with any outline, the great majority of vowels are found unessential and can be omitted. Their external position is thus a great advantage, because the learner who has got to the stage where he can omit vowels is not obliged to change the outline

---

[1] In practice there is little difficulty in learning the Pitman characters owing to the way they are grouped by shape to correspond to similarities in sound.

[2] See *Punch*, 9 June 1937; a joiner is shown replying to a wrong number on the telephone, saying 'Ah, you want Smith, J., GNGRCR, this is Smith, J., CBNTMKR.'

itself in any way, and no re-formation of the muscular reflexes involved in writing it has to be made. The practice has the further advantage that words like *photograph* and *photography*, which, owing to the differences in vowel quality between them, would look very different in a system where vowels are incorporated in the outline, are easily identifiable in Phonography.

Unmistakable outlines for words are ingeniously provided by the way vowel omission is combined with the principles of analysis we have just been discussing. The word *spy*, for example, is written $\checkmark$, the initial consonantal part being regarded as one unit. *Espy*, however, since the syllable division supplies us with an analysis of the sound group, is $\wr$ The two words are therefore quite distinct when the vowel points are omitted. *Stray* $\cap$ is in the same way distinguished from *astray* $\downarrow$

6

The state of our traditional English spelling was the first thing that drew people's attention to possibilities of improvement in our means of communication. It was chance that made shorthand Isaac Pitman's first concern, and although it is for this alone that his name is remembered, a large part of his energetic life was devoted to the other problem. The success of applying a new analysis of the language to shorthand naturally led him to believe that a new analysis might be equally successful in solving the difficulties of our spelling. He was assisted, in his long experimentation with different kinds of alphabets, by Alexander John Ellis, one of the most famous of English philologists, and on many points it is far from easy to separate their respective contributions. A detailed discussion of all they did would be highly technical and of interest to phonetic specialists only; it is sufficient to remark that Pitman's severe practicality, his refusal to be led astray by any of the current prejudices, is as apparent here as in his shorthand. Many of his followers lost sight of the purpose for which they were working—the elaboration of a reasonable English spelling—in a maze of theoretical and 'philosophical' considerations. Pitman never for a moment forgot the end to be reached,

ÐE BUK OV DJENESIS.

TƆAPTER 1.

Tᴀɴ ᴜmskwes pøktᴜmkiᴂk Niksksm kisidøgᴜp wᴂsøk ᴂk mᴂkᴜmigou,

2 Ak mᴂkᴜmigou weskedek ᴂk sigwᴂᴇk, ᴂk bø-gᴜnitpᴂk ᴇkᴜp wolkøgᴜmigegᴜ. Ak Niksksm ᴜtɕidjᴂk'midj'l etlimadjᴂsilib'nn ᴜskitpᴂktᴜgᴜ.

3 Ak Niksksm ᴇᴇp : Wosadetɕ; tøkuu wosa-degᴜp.

4 Ak Niksksm nemidøgᴜp wosadék ᴜkᴜlul-tᴜnᴜnᴜ. Ak Niksksm wedjitepkisᴂ-døgᴜp wosa-dek bøgᴜnitpᴂk iktuuk.

5 Ak Niksksm telᴜᴉidᴜgᴜp wosadék nᴂgwek, ᴂk bøgᴜnitpᴂk telᴜᴉidᴜgᴜp depkík. Tøkuu wᴇlᴂ-gᴜup ᴂk eskitpᴜugᴜup ᴜmskwesᴇwᴇ́ nᴂgwek.

6 Tøkuu Niksksm ᴇᴇp : Muuskuun ᴉitɕ lᴜugwᴇ́k samᴜugwon'l, ᴂk ᴜutɕi noᴜskᴂduutɕ sámᴜugwon'l ᴂk sámᴜugwon'l.

7 Ak Niksksm kisidøgᴜp muuskuun, ᴂk wedji noᴜskᴂdøgᴜb'nn sámᴜugwon'l ᴇbuunék muuskuun ik-tuuk ᴂk samᴜugwon'l kᴇkwᴇ́k muuskuun iktuuk. Tøkuu telisᴂgᴜp.

8 Ak Niksksm telᴜᴉidᴜgᴜp muuskuun wᴂsøk. Tøkuu welᴂgᴜup ᴂk eskitpᴜugᴜup tᴂbᴜuᴇwᴇ́ nᴂgwek.

FACSIMILE OF GENESIS I. 1–8, PRINTED IN MIKMAK
(a language spoken by a tribe of Indians in New Brunswick, Nova Scotia).

and the following quotation from his contemporary, Max Müller, Professor of Comparative Philology at Oxford, is a tribute from one of the few of his supporters who understood that this end was, after all, the universal adoption of the system:

> What I like in Mr Pitman's system of spelling is exactly what I know has been found fault with by others—namely that he does not attempt to refine too much, and to express in writing those endless shades of pronunciation, which may be of the greatest interest to the student of acoustics, or phonetics, as applied to the study of living dialects, but which for practical as well as for scientific philological purposes, must be entirely ignored. Writing was never intended to photograph spoken languages: it was meant to indicate, not to paint, sounds. If Voltaire says, 'L'écriture c'est la peinture de la voix,' he is right; but when he goes on to say, 'Plus elle est ressemblante, meilleure elle est,' I am not certain that, as in a picture of a landscape, pre-Raphaelite minuteness may not destroy the very object of the picture.

The application to other languages of the alphabets which he worked out led to the re-birth of the science of phonetics, and the reproduced passage printed, in 1860, in an alphabet Pitman had designed for Mikmak, a language of New Brunswick, must be one of the first phonetic transcriptions ever made of an unwritten language.

All modern phonetic transcription derives from the work of Pitman and Ellis, and many characters originally designed by them, such as ʒ, ʃ, ŋ, are still in use.

7

The importance of every kind of writing to civilization needs no insisting on. Our English spelling works, however clumsily, or it would not be used; but it would clearly be an advantage to have a method of writing as logically applied as possible. Many people, since Pitman and Ellis, have devoted their time and money to the problem, and to propaganda in favour of reform. But as far as actual reform goes, we are as far from it now as during Pitman's life; the Simplified Spelling Society of Great Britain, however, which was quiescent for some considerable time, is now recovering its early strength, and it is gratifying to see that Mr I. J. Pitman,[1] grandson of Sir Isaac, is closely associated with its present activities. There are rational things to be said both for and against reform (and numerous irrational ones), and this is not the place to start an argument. The important thing is that, thanks to Isaac Pitman, we now have behind us a full discussion of the possibilities, and valuable experience of how numerous different systems work in practice.

His value to all modern work in spelling reform, and his revolutionizing of shorthand construction, are not the only things for which Pitman deserves overdue recognition. A. J. Ellis and A. M. Bell, father of the inventor of the telephone, are usually regarded as the founders of the flourishing English school of Phonetics; Pitman has a right to be regarded as at least their equal, if not their superior—and Ellis and Bell would probably have been the first to admit it.

Moreover, his historical importance lies in a wider field than phonetics, stenography, or the theory of writing. In regarding visual means of communication as something which need not be left to evolve, but which can be consciously controlled, Pitman was one of the first to insist in modern times that language was made for man, not man for language.

---

[1] Now Sir James Pitman, and the originator of the Initial Teaching Alphabet—which may make reform unnecessary.

10

The recording of dialect material

I want to discuss, in this paper, not the *mechanical* recording of dialect material by machines, but its recording in writing by the field-worker; and my subject would have been indicated more precisely, perhaps, if I had called the paper 'the recording *and presentation* of dialect material'. I want to deal, in other words, with problems of notation.

What I have to say applies equally whether the field-worker himself, in the field, takes down the material; or whether he makes tape or disk recordings, brings them home, and he or someone else puts them into writing there. The procedure is the same, merely displaced and deferred in the latter case (and not done so well, probably, since we transcribe by eye to some extent as well as by ear). (What I have to say does not concern dialect investigations carried out by the postal or 'indirect' method, such as used for example by André Martinet in his study of the pronunciation of contemporary French.)

What the field-worker puts down in writing will normally be in phonetic transcription. The theory, and the practical use, of phonetic transcription has always been one of the strong points of the English (or British) school of phonetics. It has not always been used to best advantage in dialect work, however, and now that there is a revival of practical interest in British dialect studies, I want to make a special plea for more attention to notation.

There are various misunderstandings to be met with about phonetic transcription. For instance, there is the commonly stated half-truth that it does not really matter what symbols are used, as long as they are properly defined. It often *does* matter; but

Paper given at the Second International Conference of University Professors of English, held in August 1953, in Paris, and published in *Orbis*, Vol. III, 1954.

I am here mainly concerned with how symbols are put together, with *transcription* as such, and not with symbol shapes.

I regard as another misunderstanding the feeling that in dialect work the field-worker's notes, as originally taken down on the spot, are in some way sacred: that they are the *basic facts* of the study, which must on no account be tampered with. Edmond Edmont, of the Linguistic Atlas of France, sent his notes back to Gilliéron as soon as he had finished the investigation of each locality, one reason being that he would thus be prevented from yielding to the temptation to 'edit' what he had taken down.

Briefly, my point in this paper is that the field-worker's original notes are *not* the basic facts that they might appear to be; and that, as a consequence of this, they are probably not the best form for presenting results of dialect investigation to the public (I mean of course the academic public).

First, the question of the field-worker's transcriptions. The feeling which I regard as mistaken is that his notes are the raw material of the investigation in the same way as the actual utterances are, so that to tamper with them would be like faking the utterances. It is felt that they *are* the utterances, captured and transfixed for examination and analysis. The ideal trained phonetician is thus looked on as being in some way like a recording machine—his hearing of sounds automatically produces a transcription in the same way as the cutting head makes a groove in the wax. But the fact is that a transcription is not a *simple record* of an utterance; it is a *generalization about* an utterance. The utterances are the original basic facts. The field-worker's transcriptions are the first processing, the first analysis, of these facts. The transcriptions embody the initial classification of, and even theorizing about, the raw material; they are not the facts themselves.

The real raw material, the utterances, cannot of course be handled directly, because they are unique events and they are complex events. Before we can say anything about them, we must be able to treat them as made up of constituent elements, each element being the representative of a class.

This analysis, and systematization, is what all alphabetic writing does—sometimes well, sometimes badly. It represents by a linear succession of symbols in *space* something which in *time*, as normally apprehended by the listener and as felt by the speaker, is not a linear succession (the artificiality of this procedure of splitting the utterance up into small elements is much more obvious to, say, a Chinese than to us who are literate in an alphabetic system). Furthermore, it represents these elements, which are infinite in their variety, by a finite number of symbols.

The very fact, then, of putting spoken utterances into writing produces out of them a *system* with a known number of elements. Every new utterance which has to be written down is done so by being referred to this system. Phonetic transcription is a specialization of alphabetic writing, from which, in this respect, it is no different. Through it the utterances of spoken language are made tractable for linguistic investigation.

When a phonetician is listening to, and transcribing, *uninvestigated* speech, what is the system to which he refers utterances in order to write them? Whence are derived the classes to which the elements are assigned?

Whether or not it is clear to the transcriber himself what he is doing (it may not be clear), the system is a *general phonetic* one, that is to say the classes are general human categories of sound. A transcription of this kind is called *impressionistic*.

An impressionistic transcription is distinguished from what is called a *systematic* one. These are the two basic classes into which the many different types of phonetic transcription all fall. (This is not the familiar division into 'broad' and 'narrow', which are both varieties of systematic transcriptions.) In a systematic transcription, the symbols do not symbolize with reference to the general human ability to produce speech sounds, that is to say with reference to general human sound-types, but with reference to a particular language or form of speech only. The symbols are thus used more economically, and the classes of sound they represent are established on more complex grounds than phonetic similarity—on *phonemic* grounds, those who like to use that term could say.

So anything recorded in phonetic notation is not raw material but processed material, processed according to known and easily-formulated principles if it is a systematic transcription, but processed in a very individual, personal, way if it is an impressionistic one. This must necessarily be so: the categories on which an impressionistic transcription is based are *personal* categories. Since they are established on purely phonetic grounds the boundaries between them are inevitably vague and fluctuating, and each transcriber will make them where his experience, and the degree and nature of his training, dictate.

A dialect field-worker's transcriptions must be impressionistic, when he is investigating pronunciation. The utterances he is dealing with must be treated as part of an unknown language whether they are in fact or not, in so far as he must at least not assume anything about the points he is looking for. Hence his transcriptions will be personal, idiosyncratic. Gilliéron for this reason was quite right to insist on a single field-worker doing all the work. The American field-workers on the New England Atlas went to considerable trouble to make their impressionistic transcriptions as alike as possible. But even when this can be done, a transcriber's mother tongue, and the philological tradition in which he is brought up, have their effect. Thus English field-workers might be likely in their transcriptions to pay great attention to variations of vowel sounds in stressed syllables; and to pay no attention at all, for example, to varieties of *s*.

It is because of this personal, idiosyncratic character of impressionistic transcriptions that I believe they are not suitable for publication of dialect material (also because they are likely to be encumbered with diacritics). I believe the New England survey was mistaken in presenting much of its material in this form.

Dialect material, it seems to me, should always be presented in a systematic transcription. There are several varieties of systematic transcription, and the same material, I believe, can be most advantageously presented on different occasions in different ways.

It is misleading to say that types of systematic transcription vary in exactness or accuracy. A systematic transcription really consists of two parts: the symbols in the *text*, on the one hand, and the *conventions* governing their interpretation, on the other. Taken

together, these two always give the same total amount of information; but it is sometimes more convenient to have a given
item of information in the conventions, sometimes to have it in
the text. What you put into the one you take out of the other.
'Broad' and 'narrow' are not very precise terms, but they refer
to this kind of difference.

Let us consider three typical situations in which dialect material
may appear in phonetic transcription: (1) in a connected text;
(2) in isolated words and phrases in a monograph upon a particular
dialect; (3) in isolated words and phrases involved in comparison
of related dialects—on a map, for example.

(1) A basic principle in making phonetic transcriptions is that
whenever possible they should be readable. The philosopher
Thomas Hobbes once said of a work by John Wallis, Professor
of Geometry at Oxford, that it was 'so covered over with the scab
of symbols' that he had not the patience to see if it said anything
worth while. People have felt the same about linguistic works,
and especially about connected phonetic texts. This is the hardest
situation in which to make phonetic transcription readable.
Connected texts should have the maximum possible of information
in the conventions, and the bare minimum in the symbols, thus
gaining great typographical simplicity by using the fewest possible
different symbols of the simplest possible shapes. I can think of
many instances of dialect texts where this is not done.

(2) When isolated words and phrases are under discussion in a
dialect monograph, it is an advantage to have distinctions made
explicit in the symbols which, in a connected text, would be better
confined to the conventions. Here I would like to suggest the
adoption of a practice of which recent works of descriptive
linguistics from the London school, and also from Americanists,
have demonstrated the usefulness in different ways. This is the
use of two types of transcription simultaneously. A word is
transcribed first, for instance, in a way which reveals its sound-
structure; secondly, immediately after, in a way which reveals
details germane to the discussion but whose presence in the
symbols obscures the structure. The first might make clear the

phonemes, the second the allophones. The method makes for remarkable clarity of presentation.

(3) When dialects are being compared, a transcription is needed which brings out, not 'internal' distinctions, those *within* a given form of speech, but 'external' ones, between two or more forms of speech. These distinctions equally are usually stated in the conventions; but on a map, for instance, they are better explicit in the symbols. A transcription of this kind is called a *comparative* one.

I said I was not mainly concerned in this paper with symbol shapes, but I would like to add a word or two about them. They are often, in all kinds of linguistic works, hideous. The presence in the same transcription of capitals, italics, tiny letters, raised letters, diacritics, and letters from assorted founts, is nearly always unnecessary, but distressingly common. One almost suspects the existence of a feeling that the more ungraceful and untidy a transcription is the more scholarly it is—a belief that devotion to the spoken word is best expressed by neglect of the appearance of the printed page.

Let me conclude by quoting a famous mathematician, Hyman Levy: 'Notation is indeed the very life-blood of science.'

11

Pseudo-procedures in linguistics

This paper is about a rather curious, though possibly not very important, phenomenon: the fact that linguists sometimes say they do things in a certain way, when that is not the way they do them. They do not do them in the way they allege they do, because in fact they cannot. Linguists, in other words, sometimes make appeal to *pseudo-procedures*.

I intend the term 'pseudo-procedure' to be taken quite literally: I mean by it something which masquerades as a procedure, but is not one. If 'procedure' is taken to mean 'way or method of conducting an investigation', then a 'pseudo-procedure' is something which is put forward as a way of conducting an investigation, but which in fact is an impossible, or at best a completely impracticable, way—and is almost certainly known to be so by the person who puts it forward (who, apparently, is not disconcerted by this being the case).

I have at times mentioned this notion of 'pseudo-procedure' to colleagues working in linguistics, and some of them have said that pseudo-procedures are probably to be found in all subjects, and that therefore they are not really as bad as they sound. But I have never come across a convincing example in another subject, and I have reluctantly come to the conclusion—however surprising it may be—that *genuine* pseudo-procedures are peculiar to linguistics.

Let me give, by way of illustration, some instances of the kind of thing I have in mind. They will show that pseudo-procedures

Paper given to the Phonetics Postgraduate Seminar, Edinburgh University, in December 1956; and to the Linguistics Association (Great Britain), at Hull in May 1958. Published in *Zeitschrift für Phonetik, Sprachwissenschaft und Kommunikationsforschung*, Vol. XVI, 1963.

are of two sorts: in some, the alleged procedure is quite literally impossible; in others, although it may not be literally impossible, it would be so arduous and time-consuming as a way of conducting an investigation that no one in their senses would ever set out to use it. If they did, they would certainly never carry it through.

I will start with a very clear example. It is a pseudo-procedure of the second sort, one which is perhaps theoretically possible but which nobody would dream of trying to put into practice. I take it from an article by A. S. C. Ross,[1] and give it here in summary form. It is invoked by Professor Ross in order to define more satisfactorily certain linguistic concepts which, in the words of the author, at present lack 'rigid definitions'; and in particular to provide a definition of the phoneme.

The first thing which has to be done in this procedure is to arrange all the possible utterances of a normal monoglot speaker of a language into pairs, so that each utterance is paired with every other utterance; and next to select from these pairs those which are different in sense and different though similar in sound. The pairs whose difference lies only in stress or intonation, or both together, are then discarded, and from the remaining pairs, which will differ in speech-sounds, we pick out those which show *minimal* differences. Already at this stage the procedure can be seen to be a formidable one, even with computers to help (the number of possible pairs will, I suppose, run into billions). We have still, however, to repeat the whole process for every other speaker of the language before coming to the main part of the procedure, which consists of plotting in multi-dimensional domains, one acoustic and one physiological, two points for each pair of utterances, representing the speech-sounds in which they differ, and joining these pairs of points by lines. 'It is clear', writes Professor Ross, 'that we shall be confronted, in both the domains, by bundles of lines joining clusters of points.' The clusters will represent the phonemes, which can then be defined in terms of the way the clusters were arrived at.

---

[1] 'The Fundamental Definitions of the Theory of Language', *Acta Linguistica*, IV, 1944, pp. 101-6.

Whatever other flaws there may be in Professor Ross's definition, it is clear that the procedure on which it is based will never be carried out: no one is ever going to be 'confronted' by those clusters. It is strange that such a pseudo-procedure should be thought to afford a more satisfactory and 'rigid' definition of the phoneme.

My next pseudo-procedure is quite a common one, and readers will probably recognize having come across it as soon as they hear it illustrated. It is not, however, as easily recognizable as the preceding one for what it is. There is an air of reasonableness about it, and possibly many people who bring it into their writings on linguistics feel that, although it so happens that they themselves have so far never used the procedure, nevertheless they might do so at any moment, and other people probably often *have* used it. This pseudo-procedure, however, is not just impracticable: it is quite impossible.

Like the preceding pseudo-procedure, this too concerns comparing texts with small differences. A not very important instance of it occurs in André Martinet's *Phonology as Functional Phonetics*,[1] where he writes, 'If we compare two utterances like *make it* and *check it*, we know from the reactions of the person spoken to that the meaning of the one is different from that of the other'.

It is clear that Professor Martinet does not mean by these 'reactions of the person spoken to' that you ask if the utterances are different and see what the person says; the procedure rather is that you watch him on occasions when each of the two utterances are addressed to him, and see what he does. However, a moment's reflection will show that linguistics possesses *no* techniques whatever for observing and evaluating listener's reactions. If we know that the meaning of one utterance is different from that of another, we know by some other means than this alleged procedure. It is not simply that linguistics has neglected to provide itself with the necessary techniques: such techniques are not even theoretically possible. It is enough to recall that both of the utterances which we wish to compare may be received in unmoved silence—they may evoke no observable reactions at all.

[1] London, 1949, p. 3.

Professor Martinet makes nothing very much of this pseudo-procedure, and it appears to be introduced almost inadvertently. But some writers invest it with great importance. A. Cohen, for instance, in *The Phonemes of English*,[1] writes, 'throughout this phonemic study the reactions of native speakers towards (not their feelings or notions about) linguistic forms will constitute the primary source of information'. Other quotations into which the same pseudo-procedure enters are: 'We speak of significant function in all cases where a change of sound is reflected in a change of behaviour in the listener.' 'We say that the *t* of *tear* and the *w* of *wear* both have significant function, because an interchange of the two would entail different response.' *h* and ŋ 'cannot be interchanged without a change in the listener's behaviour'. Everything is presented in terms of this procedure, but can we really believe that it was 'the primary source of information'? Surely not. Yet Dr Cohen insists that 'in the following pages an attempt is made to base linguistic methods on the study of facts that can be established empirically, by observing the behaviour of speaker and listener towards linguistic forms without inter-preting it psychologically'. If, as seems probable, the facts are *not* established empirically in this way, it is curious that Dr Cohen finds it necessary to maintain that they are.

When Dr Cohen goes on to say, 'Substituting the *t* of *tomb* for the *t* of *team*, which noticeably differ from the articulatory point of view, we do not notice any difference in the behaviour of the listener', we may wonder whether yet another pseudo-procedure has not made an appearance. How *does* one substitute one allophone for another? Presumably when one talks of sub-stituting one phoneme for another, as in Dr Cohen's example of *tear* and *wear*, one takes it for granted that the appropriate changes in the phonetic environment will also be made. But if it is allo-phones that are to be interchanged, one presumes the environment is to be preserved intact. Although a well-trained phonetician can perhaps make a fair shot at doing this, there is no way of estimating the degree of his success. It may be a useful way of introducing

---

[1] The Hague, 1952.

the idea of the phoneme to beginners in phonetics, but it could scarcely be employed with confidence in making a phonemic analysis. Perhaps, however, Dr Cohen means his procedure to be one involving tape splicing, when it would not, of course, be a pseudo-procedure (though its value would still be open to doubt).

I came across a rather surprisingly frank admission of the existence of pseudo-procedures a short while ago, after a preliminary draft of this paper had been made. It is by Kenneth Pike, and is in the *Reports for the Eighth International Congress of Linguists*.[1] Pike is speaking of 'one large segment of American linguistics', and he says that when its practitioners mention procedure, 'it is likely to have reference to an idealized procedure which in fact is not used by its authors in field work. Rather procedure often takes the form of "This-is-the-way-it-should-be-done-in-principle" statements, while the authors in fact employ "short cuts" or "actual procedures" which use quite different approaches and implicit theories. It is assumed that the short cut would be illegitimate, were that all that were available to us; it is assumed that the short cut is justified, however, if it can be shown by theoretical argument, or partial success, that the fuller procedure could presumably be used if enough years were in the life span of the investigator and if he had at his command sufficient calculating machines of types presently available or conceivable.'

This may not be the only reason why some linguists feel it necessary to claim they do a thing in a certain way when in fact they do it quite differently. Another reason, I believe, is the feeling in some quarters that linguistics rather lacks prestige in the academic world, but that its prestige could be increased if it could be made to appear to be doing the same sort of thing as other subjects which undoubtedly *do* have prestige. There is a hint of this in the report that I have quoted by Pike. He says there that the strength of the particular kind of American linguistics to which he is referring lies in 'the hope it holds out of being able to treat the most complicated problems with a mathematical rigor which would bring linguists into line with the great progress

---

[1] Vol. II, p. 336 (Oslo, 1957).

achieved in the past century in disciplines where mathematical and quantitative objectivity have been achieved.' I suspect, too, that Ross means his 'rigid' definitions to have this kind of rigour. And perhaps Cohen intends the appeal to observation of listener's behaviour to produce feelings similar to those we have towards, say, Pavlov playing notes of different pitches to dogs and watching to see if they salivate or not. So it may be that pseudo-procedures are introduced for the benefit of colleagues working in other fields, rather than to impress one's fellow-linguists (and perhaps the wish to appear respectable in the eyes of natural scientists shows itself in other ways—for instance, in the rather regrettable use of the term 'language laboratory' to mean a room with some tape-recorders in it).

It is not a good thing for linguists to pretend to use procedures which are really inapplicable and belong to other disciplines. Less rigour (in any useful sense of the word) rather than more is the result. It may lead us, moreover, to be uncritical about any matters of procedure. Take, for example, the following passage in *An Outline of English Structure* by Trager and Smith (p. 35): 'Utterances having only one vowel are found to be said always with a loudness equal to the greatest loudness found in larger utterances—under the same conditions of style, emphasis, and so on.' *How* are they found to be so? I know of no procedure for ascertaining this, and it is probably not true anyway. But the statement has not been widely challenged. Pseudo-procedures are perhaps not very important in themselves, but they are symptomatic of something against which we should be on our guard.

12

Parameters and phonemes

I have defined Phonetics elsewhere as 'the study of the medium of spoken language in all its aspects', and these aspects include, of course, the process of acquiring, in childhood, the skills needed for the production of the medium, and also the failure to acquire these skills. (The acquirement of *language* as such, and the acquirement of the ability to produce ánd to receive the *medium* which carries it, are, naturally, bound up together; but it is often useful to distinguish the two things, particularly since there may be failures or breakdowns in the one which do not involve the other.)

Phonetics provides two sets of techniques which are relevant to studies of the development and disorders of speech: techniques of observation, and techniques of description. There is a close connexion between the two, of course—we tend to observe in terms of our categories of description. It is these latter that I want to talk about mostly.

Although phonetics is the study of *all* aspects of the medium, it has been dominated, in the past, as an academic subject, by one aspect—at any rate in this country, and this has left its mark on it. Phonetics has, until recently, been the handmaid of language teaching. Indeed, this has more than just left its mark on the subject—it has deeply influenced it, particularly as concerns the categories used for analysing and describing the sound of speech.

Paper given, under the title 'The Contribution of Phonetics', to an International Study Group on the Development and the Disorders of Hearing, Language and Speech in Children, held in Durham in September 1963, under the auspices of the Medical Education and Information Unit of the National Spastics Society. Published in *The Child Who Does Not Talk*, Clinics in Developmental Medicine, No. 13, London, 1964.

When people need the help of phonetics in other fields, they almost inevitably make use of the categories which have been worked out for language teaching—under the quite understandable impression that these are 'absolute' categories. But they are *not* 'absolute' categories. Phonetics today has emancipated itself from language teaching, and as an academic subject it is much wider than in the past. Its interests cover many fields. In our department at Edinburgh, language teaching occupies only a small place (possibly too small, in reaction from the past). Our main interest is in the use of phonetics in descriptive linguistics. But we co-operate closely on various research projects with departments such as physiology, physics, electrical engineering, with the College of Speech Therapists and the Dental Hospital, and with the various neurologists in different institutions in Edinburgh. And we have a special interest in speech synthesis. We have learnt that the traditional categories of analysis and description nearly always will not do in these wider fields. The making of synthetic speech especially has brought this home to us.

The Phoneme-dominated Approach

What characterizes the traditional approach to the analysis of the sound of speech? Although it is an approach which goes back long before the term 'phoneme' was invented, one could nevertheless call it a 'phoneme-dominated' approach. Speech is looked at as consisting of *segments*, each one of which represents a phoneme, which are put together to build up speech. It could equally well be called a 'building-block' approach. Its categories of description are all in these terms; they are all (or almost all) designed to describe these phoneme-representing segments, or 'speech-sounds'. True, intonation is abstracted and dealt with separately; but the syllable is ignored, and so are voice quality and rhythm. In fact the aural medium is treated as if it were closely parallel to the visual medium: as if, just as letters are put together to form written words, so phoneme-representing segments are put together to form spoken ones.

Another way of describing the traditional approach would be to call it the 'posture and glide' view of speech. Each segment is

9

envisaged as a *posture* of the vocal organs, and these postures are joined together by means of *glides*, which take us from one to the next.

However, we know—it is no new discovery—that there *are* no held postures in speech. Nothing brings this home more effectively than a slow-motion X-ray film of speech. The concept of the speech-sound as a stable (even if only momentarily stable) posture of the vocal organs is a fiction, albeit for many purposes quite a useful one.

The phoneme, which is based on this view of the sound of speech, is a construct devised to enable linguists to analyse their material *for certain purposes only*. It is not something which has a 'real existence'. The categories used for talking about speech in the 'phoneme-dominated' approach have worked very well in language teaching, and it is possible to get *some* way with them in any field. But people in all fields concerned with speech talk in terms of phonemes nowadays. It has become a vogue-word. It has also become a status-symbol—to use it shows that you are 'with it' linguistically. I constantly see the word used in situations where it is quite inappropriate. I would not think, for instance, that any of the group of doctors, teachers and therapists who assembled at Durham need ever use the term.

I do not think that the phoneme, unlike some status-symbols, is harmless; I think it is apt to confuse people's thinking about speech if they are not aware of its fictional nature. I am sure it gives rise, for example, to mistaken ideas about the perception of speech, making people think that phoneme-representing segments are perceived separately and serially—which is most unlikely. But it is not only sometimes misleading; it is often not the most efficient means for thinking about and describing speech.

A Parametric Approach

Certainly we have found these traditional categories unsatisfactory for many of the fields in which we in Edinburgh are interested. The most striking of these, perhaps, is speech synthesis. If you try to synthesize speech on a 'building-block' basis, it just doesn't work, and we do not make the machine operate by making it add together synthetic speech sounds corresponding to phoneme-representing segments. The machine, by the way, is called PAT, which stands for Parametric Artificial Talker, and the first word gives the clue as to how the machine works. *Parametric* comes from *parameter*, and the machine operates by adding together parameters, not segments. A parameter is a variable, an ingredient which is continually present but changing in value. The division of speech into phoneme-representing segments represents a division at right-angles to the time axis, whereas the division into parameters is a division parallel to the time axis.

I believe that a parametric approach is more useful for many of the purposes that we are here to discuss than a segmental approach, and that it is always a valuable supplement to a segmental approach.

The parameters of PAT are *acoustic* parameters, and I need not here go into what they are. I would like to suggest the use for our purposes of *physiological* parameters, thought of in terms of the producing mechanisms of the medium. I feel sure that these give a more realistic view of what goes on than segments do. I simply don't believe that the child, in acquiring speech, learns a series of separate units or items, which are the phoneme-representing segments, and strings them together, with varying degrees of success, at the same time superimposing on the string the rhythm of syllable-succession and the melodies of intonation. I suggest that what the child learns are patterns of movement which are quite large in time, and it learns them at first sketchily and roughly, filling them in, in more detail, as it improves. The learning of these patterns is best thought of as being in parametric terms. This is certainly better than saying, as one authority has, that the average baby under two months of age has mastered seven and a half phonemes!

What might such physiological parameters in the producing-process of the medium be? Here is a suggested list—not complete, since some of the parameters could be subdivided, and certainly some more could be added:

In the respiratory   (a) the syllable-pulse process
        system   (b) the pulse-reinforcing, or stress process

In the phonatory   (c) phonation-type control
        system   (d) on/off switching of voicing
                        (e) voice-pitch variation
In the articulatory   (f) velic valve-action
        system   (g) tongue-body movements
                        (h) tongue-tip movements
                        (i) lip movements
                        (j) jaw movements.

These parameters have, of course, to be exactly co-ordinated for the production of the medium to be correctly learnt.

I am not suggesting that we normally listen to these parameters. We *hear* the medium as a single unanalysed continuing noise, fluctuating in quality. We *listen*, perhaps, in terms of three parameters representing three expressive systems:

  (i) articulatory patterns,
 (ii) intonation patterns,
(iii) register ('voice quality') variations.

The three systems operate in speech quite independently of each other, and they are listened to *as language*, plus indications of mood, character, and so on.

But we can *learn* to listen in terms of the physiological parameters enumerated above, or even sub-divisions of them, so that failures to master the medium can be described in their terms, and so can the development of speech in the child. It is almost impossible to describe babbling in terms of phoneme-representing segments (though attempts have been made to do so), but it can be done parametrically.

This is put forward very tentatively. What we badly need is research at the postgraduate level, in a phonetics department, into the problems of the learning of speech and of speech pathology. I have in mind, in this connexion, not only the contribution which phonetics can make to such research, but also the contribution which such research can make to the development of phonetics, for it has been found that the study of speech in one set of circumstances and for one set of purposes is always illuminating for the study of it in all others.

13

Direct palatography

I use the expression '*direct* palatography' to mean the investigation of articulatory movements by means of marks made directly on the roof of the mouth, as distinct from the more usual technique which employs an artificial palate. The two methods of investigation seem to have been independently discovered. We owe both of them to dentists interested in oral deformities, and they were both first described in print during the seventies of last century. One originated in England, and the other in America. Direct palatography was slightly the earlier, and a London dentist, J. Oakley Coles (1845-1906) of Wimpole Street, was its inventor and the first to practise it.[1] Coles had found that he was handicapped in treatment of defects of the palate by lack of information on how to teach his patients to speak correctly (he seems to have been ignorant of the extensive phonetic literature which existed at the time). He was thus led to work out, in the shape of his direct palatography technique, 'a plan for ascertaining more accurately the physiology of speech', and he made the method public, after a couple of years of experiment, in a paper read to a meeting of the Odontological Society of Great Britain on 5 February 1872.[2] His procedure involved taking, as a preliminary, an impression of his upper jaw back to the posterior wall of the pharynx and including the soft palate and fauces, and another impression of his lower jaw with the tongue at rest. From these impressions he made drawings of the interior of his mouth, one

---

[1] Coles later took orders and became Vicar of All Saints, Upper Norwood.
[2] See the Society's *Transactions*, Vol. IV, pp. 110-23, London, 1872. The text of the paper is accompanied by twenty-six coloured plates.

Published in *Zeitschrift für Phonetik und allgemeine Sprachwissenschaft*, Vol. X, 1957.

of the upper jaw and one of the lower jaw. These drawings were reproduced lithographically in a number of copies. His method was then to paint his hard and soft palate and the surfaces of his upper teeth with a mixture of gum and flour, so that he was able, after 'sharply articulating a letter', as he put it, to observe where the mixture had been removed and therefore what the point of contact between the articulating organs had been. The point of contact was recorded in red on the two lithographs, being shown both for the tongue and for the roof of the mouth.

Coles's technique was most original, but his ignorance of phonetics prevented him from using it with profit. His experiments were apparently made by saying the *name* of each letter: he explained in his paper that 'the names given to the different letters may . . . be taken as epitomizing the parts involved in their production'. Needless to say this tended to produce strange results, and sometimes the articulations he records are quite inexplicable, as when P and B reveal considerable contact between tongue and upper gums behind the front teeth. However, Coles did not claim to have carried out a complete investigation of English sounds, but only to be demonstrating 'a new mode of observation'.

A few investigators (Grützner, Techmer, Lenz, Rousselot, for example) used direct palatography for linguistic research during the fifteen or so years following the appearance of Coles's paper. Meanwhile, however, Norman W. Kingsley (1829-1913), a well-known New York dental surgeon, had by 1879 developed and made public the technique of the artificial palate, and had produced by its means excellent palatograms of English articulations.[1] (It is interesting that Kingsley may have been anticipated in the invention of this technique by Erasmus Darwin, the grandfather of Charles Darwin and of Francis Galton. Darwin describes in his *Temple of Nature* (1803), a method he had devised for investigating the formation of vowel sounds. He inserted cylinders, rolled from

---

[1] See *The New York Medical Journal*, July 1879. See also Kingsley's *Oral Deformities* (London, 1880), particularly Part IV. (Kingsley lectured to the Odontological Society in London in 1864 on the uses of false vela and obturators in cases of cleft palate; Coles had not at that time joined the Society.)

tinfoil, into the mouth, and 'found by the impressions made on them, in what part of the mouth each of the vowels was formed'. Darwin does not make his method entirely clear in detail, but at least the *principle* of palatography may be said to be present in it.) Although it was some years after Kingsley first made his technique public before it became known to linguists, as soon as it did so it rapidly established itself, and it eventually proved much the more popular method in the history of palatography. Rousselot, for example, soon came to prefer it to the earlier direct technique, which in fact was little used after 1890. Scripture's *Elements of Experimental Phonetics* (1902) gives a very full account of nineteenth-century use of the artificial palate for linguistic work (see pp. 296 ff.).

It is worth while drawing attention, however, to a very successful, though not well known, instance of the employment of direct palatography made after the method of the artificial palate had been generally adopted. In 1899 Dr S. W. Carruthers obtained his M.D. at Edinburgh University with a thesis entirely devoted to palatography. It was entitled 'A contribution to the Mechanism of Articulate Speech', and was published in the *Edinburgh Medical Journal* in 1900 in three instalments, which were reprinted and issued in the same year in the form of a booklet of fifty-eight pages, copiously illustrated, with the same title as the original thesis. The work is not very accessible, and does not appear in the bibliographies where one would expect to find it. Although it occasionally seems that Dr Carruthers was unaware of the work of some of his contemporaries, his thesis is a model of physiological phonetics. He had read Coles, and had, in addition, received a good grounding in phonetics from John Wyllie (author of *The Disorders of Speech*, 1894), then lecturer in Medicine at Edinburgh, and later Professor of Medicine there from 1900 to 1915. Dr Carruthers made a survey of all English sounds, and some others, by means of direct palatography, and recorded his results, in the same way as Coles did, in drawings showing both tongue and palate contacts; he included lip contacts also. G. Noel-Armfield, in the third (1924) and subsequent editions of his *General Phonetics*, devotes considerable space to Dr Carruthers's work; he thought it would be of great advantage to the study of phonetics if it could be reprinted. This was unfortunately never done, but Noel-Armfield reproduces in his book a number of Dr Carruthers's palatograms and 'linguagrams', as the former calls them.

In spite of this illustration of how successfully direct palatography could be used by a skilled investigator, it has been a neglected technique for most of this century. Very recently, however, there has been a revival of interest in it in two different places. It is an agreeable coincidence that one of these places should be Edinburgh University, in the Department of Phonetics.[1] The other is the Phonetic Institute at the University of Uppsala. The use of the technique in the latter place has been well described by Claes Witting in *Studia Linguistica* ('New Techniques in Palatography', 1953). It is the purpose of the present article to say something about the technique as developed at Edinburgh.

Like the Uppsala technique, the Edinburgh one consists essentially of photographing the roof of the mouth as reflected in a mirror, and this is done by means of apparatus devised by Mr James Anthony, of the staff of the Edinburgh Phonetics laboratory. Mr Anthony has given an account of his apparatus and its use in an article in *The Science Technologists' Association Bulletin*,[2] and I shall refer here only briefly to the mechanical details of it. The apparatus is made up of four parts: (1) a device for spraying a marking mixture on to the articulating organs; (2) mirrors for inspection and to provide an image for photographing; (3) illumination; (4) a camera. The investigator, sitting in front of the apparatus, sprays his hard and soft palate

---

[1] When experiments on direct palatography were started there in 1951, it was in ignorance of the earlier efforts of Dr Carruthers. It is a matter of great satisfaction to me and to my colleagues that Dr Carruthers, now resident in the South of England, has since been able to visit the Phonetics Department and inspect the work in progress there, over fifty years after the publication of his own palatographic researches carried out in the same university. I am indebted to Dr Carruthers, who knew Coles, for information concerning the latter's later life. (Since this article was written a biographical note on Coles, by Dr Lilian Lindsay, has appeared in the *British Dental Journal* for 16 August 1955.)

[2] 'New Method for Investigating Tongue Positions of Consonants', October-November 1954, pp. 2-5.

and the lingual surfaces of his upper teeth with a mixture of charcoal and powdered chocolate. Then, after making the articulation which is to be investigated, he leans forward slightly so that a mirror, which is suitably shaped, slips into his mouth, into the interior of which a powerful light is directed. The 'wipe-off', or area of contact, on his palate is then visible to him, reflected from the mirror in his mouth on to another mirror mounted opposite (he will also use this view for first checking the accuracy of the spraying). At least two other people, one behind and one in front, can get a comfortable view of the palate beside the investigator himself. If the latter is satisfied with the results obtained from that particular utterance, he can photograph the image of his palate in the mirror by means of the camera, which is facing him. The apparatus is neither very expensive nor very difficult to construct.

Two very evident advantages of direct palatography over the artificial palate technique are at once apparent: first, it is possible to record the contacts of the tongue against the surfaces of the teeth; and second, and more important, it is possible to investigate back vowels and velar consonants. There are other advantages. The most obvious is that direct palatography avoids the interference with articulatory movements that the artificial palate inevitably entails (though the latter is not, for a practised research worker in phonetics, such an encumbrance as it might at first seem to be). A less immediately obvious advantage is that people who have false teeth can practise direct palatography, whereas it is difficult—in fact usually impossible—for them to use the method of the artificial palate. They can investigate articulations while their dental plate is in position just as easily, by the former method, as can people who have only their own teeth.

Another advantage of the method is its simplicity. A certain amount of practice is needed for its most successful use (rather less, perhaps, than is needed to learn to manage an artificial palate): it takes some time to acquire the trick of spraying the whole roof of the mouth rapidly and economically; and some research workers find that their salivation is excessive at first and needs to be controlled. Once mastered, however, the technique of direct palatography is a most expeditious implement of research, and the experienced 'palatographer' can take forty or more photopalatograms of his own articulations in an hour. Moreover, he can work entirely by himself, without any assistance.

One final advantage should be mentioned, and that is the value of the technique not only for research, but also for teaching. Articulatory movements which are not visible are not easy to grasp for beginners in phonetics, whose kinesthetic sense is usually still undeveloped for the tongue. Descriptions of these movements can be made more real and less purely theoretical by means of palatography (which must be active participation in palatography, not just the exhibition of other people's palatograms); but the labour and expense involved in making artificial palates for each member of a large class would normally rule its use out. At the Phonetics Department of Edinburgh University, however, a considerable number of beginners in general phonetics is taught every year, and direct palatography is found a very practicable and a most valuable aid in their instruction. (Inspection of the palate by means of the mirrors is usually sufficient for teaching purposes; photographs are only taken when a permanent record of the wipe-off resulting from a particular utterance is required.)

The Anthony apparatus is already proving its usefulness in other than purely linguistic fields; it is employed, for example, in the Orthodontics Department of the Edinburgh Dental Hospital. Nevertheless, there is, of course, room for improvement in various ways. It is hoped that a means will be obtained of overcoming the distortion produced by the angle of the mirror (see Witting, op. cit., p. 59), and it is likely that a more suitable camera will shortly be found. The illumination is not perfect. The next big problem to be tackled is the recording of the contact area on the *tongue*: the making of 'linguagrams' (or, preferably, *glossograms*— the term used by Heinrich Witthöft in connexion with the technique he made public in 1938: see *Archiv für Sprach- und Stimmheilkunde*). This still offers many difficulties, but is a necessary complement to successful palatography.

14

On writing and the phoneme: two reviews

(i) On Writing

It is something of a paradox that, although Mr Mitchell and Miss Lambert are here[1] exclusively concerned with written symbols and the techniques of their production, yet these two books will be of considerable interest to phoneticians, who, it is usually said, should regard the written word as not their business. The paradox, though, is perhaps not so great after all, for it is tempting to think that the study of spoken sounds and the study of written shapes really form one single subject. Phonetics has always, in this country at least, been in practice a wider and more human subject than most definitions would make it, and phoneticians have often recognized (perhaps not very explicitly) that the mediums, or vehicles, through which language is given physical existence cannot adequately be considered apart from each other—except as physical events with no linguistic implications. Might not phonetics be redefined as *the study of letters* (using the latter term in its early grammatical sense[2])? At any rate, these two books show clearly what a serious limitation is placed on linguistic study by an allegedly behaviourist view of language, currently fashionable in some quarters, which would make it consist solely of 'the noise you make with your face'.[3] A written

---

[1] *Writing Arabic: A Practical Introduction to Ruq'ah Script*, by T. F. Mitchell. London: Oxford University Press, 1953.

Introduction to the Devanagari Script, by H. M. Lambert. London: Oxford University Press, 1953.

[2] See Ch. VII.

[3] L. Bloomfield in *Language*, Vol. XII (1936), p. 139.

These book reviews, which are slightly abbreviated here, appeared in *Le Maître Phonétique*, the first in 1954 (pp. 32-4) and the second in 1950 (pp. 31-3).

symbol is an 'inscribed gesture', as much a part of linguistic behaviour as the audible gestures of spoken language. The theoretical importance of these books is that they give a convincing and concrete demonstration of the linguistic value of the study of written symbols; and the demonstration could only have been given by people trained in the discipline of linguistic phonetics.

In addition to being of great theoretical interest, these two works are models of what practical textbooks should be: they are admirably planned and illustrated, and will be of the greatest use to students of the languages concerned. It is remarkable that contemporary linguistic pedagogy should insist so strongly on the importance of a good pronunciation in talking, but neglect so completely the matter of a good hand in writing. Language textbooks normally provide plenty of pronunciation drills, but no instructions on the script, and many language teachers must at times have been struck by this incongruous treatment of the two mediums. As Mr Mitchell says, 'there exists a definite hiatus at the beginning of all language instruction which a systematic study of written forms would do much to remove'. This hiatus is quite obvious even when fellow users of the roman alphabet are concerned; it is even more apparent with a language normally written in some other script. Its existence is difficult to account for, since, as Professor Firth points out in his foreword to Miss Lambert's book, 'the practice of the hand is an obligation no less compelling than that of the tongue and both are expressions not only of courteous relations but of disciplined knowledge'. Mr Mitchell and Miss Lambert show, in these books, how systematic instruction in the production of written symbols can best be made available to the language learner. It is striking how similar the techniques, both descriptive and normative, evolved by phonetics for dealing with spoken sounds, are to the techniques applied in the works under review to written shapes.

Although it is etymologically justifiable (as Professor Firth has elsewhere observed) to speak of the Arabic *alphabet*, the Arabic writing system is nevertheless not an *alphabetic* one as we understand the term. Mr Mitchell makes clear that 'the Arabic vowels are not letters'; they are diacritics, and the writing system is syllabic. It is a very difficult script. 'The Arabs', Mr Mitchell points out, 'have ever paid little heed to the problems of the normal reader': theirs is a scholars' writing system, rather than one to be used for combating illiteracy. In Arabic writing 'the significant pattern is that of the word rather than the letter'. This importance of the word-contour as a whole is largely what makes the script so difficult to learn and to expound. The book describes each letter first in its isolated form, and then in the various forms it assumes in the word-contour. The learner is recommended, however, to master all the isolated forms before proceeding to the combined ones, though he is reminded that 'just as in speech, so in written Arabic the greatest profit is perhaps derived from study of the methods of joining the letter-isolates. Present-day emphasis on syntagmatic or "horizontal" study and analysis in phonetics and phonology, is equally justified in the treatment of written forms.'

The two books deal with very different writing systems (though the Devanagari too is a syllabary), and they are two very different books (though the fact that both authors are members of the staff of the School of Oriental and African Studies in London is apparent in a common outlook and vocabulary). Miss Lambert's is divided into five sections, treating respectively of the writing of Sanskrit, Hindi, Marathi, Gujarati, and Bengali. Each section follows the same plan: there are chapters on the arrangement of the syllabary; the description of the characters; the formation of conjunct characters; and a prose text is added. Each section is to a great extent self-contained, which involves a certain amount of repetition, but makes it easy to compare the writing of the four modern languages with each other and with Sanskrit. All have fundamentally the same writing system, but they differ in the shapes and realizations of the characters. Miss Lambert's clear exposition shows why it was that Sir William Jones valued the Devanagari so highly.

Respect for written shapes is abundantly demonstrated in the production, as well as the writing, of these books, which are a pleasure to handle. Both authors and publisher are to be

congratulated. The usefulness of a 'good hand' can be as great
as that of a good pronunciation; and the study of what constitutes
a good hand, and of the structure of writing systems, is as
linguistically illuminating as the study of sounds and phonemes.
It is very much to be hoped that textbooks on other scripts will
be forthcoming inspired by the same principle of analysis and
exposition.

(ii) On the Phoneme

Some technical terms, once they have been coined, seem so
indispensable that it is difficult to imagine how people got along
without them. Perhaps 'phoneme' is one of these, for the idea
is undoubtedly older than the word—some would claim that
the idea goes back to the invention of the alphabet, and is
implicit, not only in broad transcriptions, but in all alphabetic
writing. However that may be, the notion lacked an explicit
label until not very long ago, though during the comparatively
brief period of its existence the term has attained remarkably
wide currency. Daniel Jones, through his teaching and writings,
has done as much as anyone to popularize it. The present full-
length exposition of his views on the nature and use of the
phoneme[1] has long been awaited, and will be read with the
greatest interest by all who are concerned with linguistic theory.

The book does not, of course, contain any surprises, for the
use which Jones makes of the concept is familiar to phoneticians
the world over; but it does provide a more detailed consideration
than he has previously given of the many problems of the analysis
and notation of speech with which phoneme theory must deal,
and the points he makes are illustrated by an astonishingly wide
range of examples. Jones's approach is severely matter-of-fact,
and it is clear on every page that the author's main preoccupations
have been practical language teaching and the elaboration of
transcriptions and orthographies. It is significant that Jones
regards phoneme theory as an integral part of phonetic science,

---

[1] *The Phoneme: Its Nature and Use*, by Daniel Jones. Cambridge: W. Heffer
and Sons Ltd, 1950.

through which exclusively, he claims, his conclusions have been reached. The manner in which he uses the phoneme does not lead to any separation of 'phonemics' from phonetics.

The value of an explicit label for this old notion is fairly generally admitted: the term has provided a brief and convenient way of stating a variety of things about speech and writing; and its uses, and usefulness, are made amply clear by Jones. It has, however, revealed itself to be more fertile of disputes than any other topic in the whole of linguistics. The usefulness of phonemes may be agreed on, but their nature is not, and the word has become a focal point for what Sapir has called 'phonetic metaphysics'. Daniel Jones has, in the past, engaged little in these controversies on phonemic fundamentals, and those who hope to find him taking sides in the present work will be disappointed. Most views of the nature of the phoneme might be said to be either of a *realist* or of a *nominalist* type, and Jones, it is true, at times appears to incline to one of these, and at times to the other. When, for example, he considers the 'instinctive feelings' of the native speaker a possible guide in phonemic analysis, the implication is that a phoneme is something which has existence in a language (or in a speaker). When, on the other hand, he says that it is, on occasion, possible to *select* the phoneme to which a sound shall be assigned, he would seem to be taking the view that phonemes are imposed on language from without by the investigator. Jones's 'physical' conception of the phoneme, however, as a 'family of sounds' is, in intention, non-committal, and he does not find it necessary to say what it is that ultimately holds the family together as a unit. He demonstrates, in fact, that it is possible to make good use of the word 'phoneme' without being committed to any fixed views as to the nature of the entity to which it refers.

Though the reader, on finishing the book, will probably have little doubt about the usefulness of the term 'phoneme', he may not, after all, be convinced of its indispensability. When Messrs Pitman and Ellis wrote, over a hundred years ago, that in their 'phonotypy' or phonetic writing 'no letter represents absolutely the same sound, except in conjunction with the same letters', they were saying a good deal of what people now use the term 'phoneme' to express; and it is tempting to take Jones's similar sentence: 'the values to be attached to the letters in phonetic transcriptions are not absolute but must always be interpreted in the light of the phonetic context' as a summary of much of his present book.

There have been more than a few occasions when discussions about the phoneme have become heated, but this is most certainly not an argumentative work. Those who are confirmed adherents of rival conceptions of the phoneme will find their views discussed briefly and tolerantly, and little further notice taken of them; they will also find abundant material on which to test their views, and fully illustrated accounts of those many cruces for which any phoneme theory must have a solution. The author warns us not to regard his opinions as dogmatic or final pronouncements, and not to take them as embodying an orthodoxy. He modestly claims no more for his approach than that it 'works well in practical language study', and the many who have followed him in so using it will testify that that is true.

15

A Scottish vowel

In the speech of many speakers of 'educated' or 'polite' Scots, a vowel phoneme is to be found which does not seem to have been noticed up to now by phoneticians (my attention was first drawn to it by Mr A. J. Aitken, of the *Dictionary of the Older Scottish Tongue*). This vowel may most typically be heard in the first syllable of the word *never*, but it occurs in a number of other words also. It is not explicable as an allophone of any other vowel phoneme in educated Scots. Its distribution is, nevertheless, curiously restricted (which may be why it has escaped notice for so long).

The quality of this vowel is usually about half way between Cardinal Vowels 2 and 3, and it is considerably centralized. The lips are neutral. It varies, of course, from speaker to speaker, as do all the vowels of educated Scots; it is often indistinguishable from the sound used by many English people—myself, for instance —in this same word *never* (which is possibly another reason why it has escaped notice). It is, however, kept distinct by Scots speakers from the vowel in the first syllable of, for example, *sever*, which is a fully front vowel and close to Cardinal 3. *Never* and *sever* do not, therefore, provide a rhyme. It is also kept distinct from the vowel in the first syllable of *shiver*, which though equally centralized is much higher. It has so far been identified only in stressed syllables.

The following are some of the words in which the vowel is commonly heard: *bury, devil, earth, eleven, ever, every, heaven, McKenzie, never, next, seven, seventy, shepherd, together, twenty*. It is found sporadically in a large number of other words (in many of which, as in many of the preceding list, it is followed by the

From *Le Maître Phonétique*, 1954, pp. 23-4.

consonant *v*). Its distribution varies with different speakers, and it is possible that this has a regional basis. The easiest way of testing for its occurrence in a given word is by means of possible rhyming pairs; thus *heaven* can be tested by *leaven*, *next* by *vexed*, *shepherd* by *leopard*, *earth* by *berth*, and so on. If the words in each pair do not rhyme, the first may be presumed to have this extra vowel, since *leaven*, *vexed*, *leopard*, *berth* seem never to have it. (It is worth noting that a speaker who has this vowel in *earth* very probably therefore has four different vowels where R.P. has only one: *birth*, *earth*, *berth*, *worth* may all contain different vowels.) A minimal pair is provided, for some speakers, by the words *bury* and *berry*.

Index

140INDEX

Carruthers, S. W., 127-8
chest-pulse, defined, 16-17
Chinese, word symbols in, 88, 90, 99,
Classe, A., 27   [110
Cohen, A., 117-18, 119
Coleridge, *Christabel*, 21-2
Coles, J. Oakley:
  biographical note on, 128n;
  direct palatography technique, 125-6
commentary on a news reel, 1, 2
Comenius, 48
consonants:
  in Lodwick's alphabet, 51-3;
  in Lodwick's shorthand, 49;
  in phonematic structure of feet, 31;
  in Tucker's alphabet, 63;
  Pitman's treatment of, 103-4
conversation:
  and spoken prose, 1-9;
  apparent incompleteness of, 8;
  as a category of spoken language, 2;
  defined, 2, 3;
  development of monologue and
    reading aloud from, 2-3;
  difference between spoken prose and,
    4, 5-6, 7-9;
  finding of examples for examination,
    3, 4-5;
  foot and syllable-quantity in, 24;
  forms of, 3-4;
  intonation in, 6, 7;
  listening to, 7;
  meaningless words and phrases in,
    8-9;
  non-fluency in, 8;
  outside view of, 5;
  pauses in, 7-8;
  phonetic notation for recorded, 7;
  recording of, 4-5;
  repetition in, 8, 9;
  rhythmic basis of, 18;
  segments of, 8;
  silence in, 8;
  stammers in, 8;

structure of, 5-7;
study of, 9;
tempo in, 7;
time units in, 29;
visual participation in, 5;
written texts of, 6-7
coughs, in conversation, 7
Cross, M. W., 27
cross-examining a witness, 1

Daines, Simon, 77n, 78, 84
Dalgarno, George, 47-8
Danes, John, 80n, 84
Darwin, Erasmus, 126-7
de Laguna, G. A., 37n
Devanagari, learning the script of,
dialect(s):   [131-4
  comparison of, 113;
  defined, 11;
  grammar of, 11;
  G.W.'s views on, 57;
  material, presentation of, 108;
  material, recording of, 108-13;
  pronunciation of, 11;
  speakers, 12;
  syllable-quantity in, 34;
  syntax of, 11;
  variation of intonation patterns in,
    38;
  vocabulary and, 11
dictionaries:
  pronouncing, 68;
  Spence's, 69-70, 71
digraphs:
  G.W.'s, 56;
  in *The Needful Attempt*, 58
direct palatography, *see* palatography
Dobson, E. J., 45
drilling a squad, 1

Edinburgh, University of:
  research into direct palatography
    techniques, 128-30;
  research into synthetic speech, 122-3

spelling–*cont.*:
  Crusonean, 74-5;
  etymology and, 95;
  G.W.'s views on, 54-7;
  ideograms and, 101;
  in *The Needful Attempt*, 58-60;
  less letters in words, 55-6;
  new letters, 55-6, 63-5, 69, 70, 72;
  phonetic, 58;
  Pitman's interest in, 94-5, 106-7;
  Pitman's system and, 104-7;
  pronunciation and, 54-5, 57, 58, 61,
    95, 98;
  reform, 54-60, 73-5, 98, 106;
  Society of Great Britain, Simplified,
  speech-sounds and, 82-4;   [106;
  Spence's views on, 73-5;
  the letter and, 82-4
Spence, Thomas:
  Dictionary, 69-70, 71;
  life of, 68-9;
  new alphabet, 69, 70, 72;
  projected reprint of the Bible, 74-5;
  spelling reforms, 73-5;
  *Supplement to the History of Robinson
    Crusoe*, 74;
  The Grand Repository, 68-73
spoken language:
  as audible gestures, 131-2;
  categories of, 2-3;
  defined, 1;
  kinds of, 1-2;
  linguistics, phonetics and, 4;
  listening to, 5;
  phonetics and, 4;
  teaching of, 9;
  writing and, 36, 97-8
spoken prose:
  conversation and, 1-9;
  difference between conversation and,
  in novels and plays, 4;   [4, 5-6, 7-9;
  intonation in, 7;
  linguistic investigation of, 4;
  listening to, 5-6;

  pauses in, 7-8;
  segments of, 8;
  stammers in, 8;
  teaching of, 9;
  tempo in, 7
stammers, 7, 8
Standard English:
  and the accent-bar, 13, 15;
  as a language, 10, 11;
  defined, 10;
  in England, 10, 11;
  pronunciation of, 11;
  received pronunciation of, 11-15, 34;
  syllable-quantity in, 34;
  with an accent, 10, 11, 12, 14, 15, 34;
  without an accent, 10, 11, 12;
  writing of, 10
Steele, Joshua:
  contribution to phonetics, 42-4;
  measure of speech, 36, 38-41, 43;
  melody of speech, 36-8, 41;
  Monboddo, Garrick and, 35-44;
  origin of notation, 35-6;
  Prosodia Rationalis, 35;
  stress-timed rhythm of English, 26n;
  symbols used by, 41;
  use of notation, 40, 41;
  views of intonation, 36-8, 42-3
stenography:
  early systems of, 95-6;
  need for speed in, 87, 91, 95-6;
  significance of Pitman system, 101-4;
  success of Pitman system, 94
Stetson, R. H., 77n
stress:
  marking of, in Lodwick's alphabet,
    53;
  silent, 20-5, 41-2;
  syllable-quantity and, 28;
  syllables, 67;
  -timed rhythm, 17-18, 21-2, 26, 33-4
stress-pulses:
  defined, 17;
  isochronous, 28;

A series bringing together writings from the different fields of linguistics, language study, and language teachin, methodology and materials.

10. *David Abercrombie*   **Studies in Phonetics & Linguistics**

Professor Abercrombie is widely known for his lucid contributions to many areas of phonetics, including the analysis of English speech, the relations between poetry and everyday discourse, the development of instrumental phonetics, transcription and the choice of symbols, and above all, the creation of a general theory of phonetics. This volume of his papers, collected from widely separated journals, not only illustrates several of these themes, but also examines other aspects of applied linguistics, such as field-study techniques, the visual symbolization of speech, and palatography.

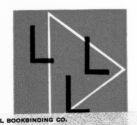

Oxford University Press

ISBN 0 19 437023 2